THE
RIVER
IN ME

*Verses of
Transformation*

COLLECTED
POEMS

THE
RIVER
IN ME

SISTER DANG NGHIEM, MD
Foreword by James R. Doty, MD

PARALLAX PRESS
Berkeley, California

Parallax Press
2236B Sixth Street
Berkeley, CA 94710
parallax.org

Parallax Press is the publishing division of Plum Village Community of
Engaged Buddhism
© 2024 by Plum Village Community of Engaged Buddhism
All rights reserved

Cover design by Katie Eberle
Text design by Maureen Forys, Happenstance Type-O-Rama
Author photograph © by Plum Village Community of Engaged Buddhism
Printed in the United States of America

Content guidance: These poems explore aspects of healing from complex
PTSD and contain references to childhood neglect, sexual abuse, and self-
harm. Please read with care.

Library of Congress Cataloging-in-Publication Data available upon request

Print ISBN: 9781952692840
E-book ISBN: 9781952692864

1 2 3 4 5 VERSA 28 27 26 25 24

MIX
Paper from
responsible sources
FSC® C005010

In loving memory of
John Earl Seaver
(1965–1999)

. . . need i say forgive me my love when i may take leave of this world; check out for a while. i know what i do, and i know not what i do.

SEPTEMBER 16, 1997

two lovers parting ways,
our heart may not split,
if we live in the center
of our original nature.

—JOHN EARL SEAVER

Contents

PART 2. FEATHER ON A MIDDAY
Poems after Monastic Ordination (2000–present)

Foreword

Welcome to the profound world of Sister Dang Nghiem, where every poem is a step toward healing, understanding, and unconditional love.

In this deeply moving collection of poetry, Sister Dang Nghiem offers us a window into a soul that has traversed darkness and emerged with a message of light. Her journey, marked by leaving war-torn Vietnam as a refugee speaking little English, the profound scars of childhood trauma, the healing embrace of medicine, and finally, the serene path of Buddhism, is nothing short of remarkable. Each poem is a testament to her resilience—a delicate weave of pain, hope, compassion, and transcendence.

As you turn these pages, you will encounter the raw honesty of Sister Dang Nghiem's early struggles as she unfolds the vivid memories of a young girl grappling with experiences no child should ever face. Yet it is not despair that defines these verses, but the incredible strength of the human spirit. Sister Dang Nghiem's journey through the medical profession and the loss of a partner is an endeavor to heal others even as she seeks healing for herself, underscored by her profound empathy and commitment to service.

The transition from physician to Buddhist nun is a poignant narrative of self-discovery and spiritual awakening. In her poetry, Sister Dang Nghiem invites us to experience not only the world of her childhood but also her world of contemplation. Her verses resonate with the peace and clarity she has found, offering solace and guidance to others on their own journeys.

This collection is more than just poetry; it is a beacon of hope and a source of comfort. It reminds us of the resilience of the human heart and the transformative power of forgiveness and compassion.

The River in Me is not merely to be read; it is to be experienced, cherished, and shared. As you immerse yourself in her words, may you find your own inner strength and peace. May her journey inspire you to navigate your own challenges with grace and to seek the healing and enlightenment that lies within us all.

JAMES R. DOTY

James R. Doty, MD, is the founder and director of the Stanford Center for Compassion and Altruism Research and Education (CCARE) at Stanford University School of Medicine, senior editor of The Oxford Handbook of Compassion Science, *and* New York Times *bestselling author of* Mind Magic: The Neuroscience of Manifestation and How It Changes Everything.

Preface

As a child in Vietnam, I often sang made-up songs to comfort myself and to express the suffering and sadness I was experiencing. Much later, after I came to the United States as a teenager, I found myself drawn to English literature and writing courses. Writing poetry offered me another pathway, a different modality to reflect upon my life and make sense of the circumstances that had driven me to make up songs in my head all those years ago. Though creating poems was cathartic and liberating in many ways, when I became a Buddhist nun in my early thirties, my life and my writing style completely changed.

This volume contains two distinct collections of poems: those written in the period from 1989–1999, before my monastic ordination, and those written afterward, from 2000 until the present. Looking back at the poems I wrote before I was ordained, I see deep aspirations for reconciliation, peace, and freedom in the midst of the drama and trauma of my life's events. I see valuable insights into my circumstances. I also recognize, however, that the way out of suffering was not yet clear to me. My thinking was still caught in romantic notions, attachment, and sorrow. Perhaps my writing before was beautiful, but it went in circles.

You can be a great writer, but this in itself won't save your life. It is the practice of mindfulness that has helped me save my life; this practice is the reason I choose to publish this collection of poetry now, more than three decades after first beginning to write. In the Zen tradition in general, and in the Plum Village tradition founded by my teacher, Zen Master Thich Nhat Hanh, specifically, we write poems called "insight gathas," verses that convey our deepest aspirations and point the way toward happiness. As a nun, I have the opportunity to confront the pain and misery of my past, and the Plum Village mindfulness practices of stopping and deep looking have helped me transform, heal, and release much of my suffering. As I began to see a way out of my internal prison, the insights arising from practicing mindfulness made their way into my poems, changing the quality and purpose of my writing. Instead of simply writing about suffering as I had previously, my words began to share a way out of suffering. Although stylistic changes came with my expanding and shifting vocabulary as I devoted myself to a life of practice in the monastic community, it is the shift toward transformation and freedom that I think make these poems worth sharing. The healing that is evident in the second half of this collection is a healing that is available to you, too.

These two poetry collections, presented here as one, feel like the before and after stages of a commitment to heal. This juxtaposition, I find, illuminates the metamorphosis of my writing style, attitude, and insights. Writing poetry or indeed any art or reflective practice can be a powerful mindfulness practice, illuminating both the mud and lotuses of life, and it is in this spirit that I am inspired to write today. There are, of course, many writers and people who are much more capable than I am of eloquently expressing themselves, but I hope to offer something helpful nonetheless: insights expressed in simple, honest ways, based on direct experience, that may allow us to see a way out of our suffering.

May these verses support your healing.

SISTER DANG NGHIEM
Deer Park Monastery
Spring, 2024

PART 1.
HERE LIE
MY SHADOWS

*Poems before
Monastic Ordination
(1989–1999)*

GRANDMA

Once I asked if you loved me.
You laughed and questioned who would love
My dog-born face.
Then you turned away to cough,
And I awkwardly reached for your back.

Once I kissed your cheeks and tasted
Grooves of your skin between my lips.
You hit my teenage pimple with your quivering fist.
I laughed and dabbed my tears.

And the day I left you for America,
You placed my hands in your spread-out palm.
You spit chewed betel juice and circled it slowly on my hands,
Saying: "This is to help you not to miss Grandma too much."
You refused to go to the airport.

I was sixteen and a half when I left Vietnam with a five-dollar bill
And a few English greeting phrases.
From America, I wanted to send you newspapers and Smitty's
    plastic bags,
So you could sell them by the gram;
People threw them away here.

I wanted to send you a waterbed, so you could float gently to
    your sleep;
Your seventy-five-year-old body would not have to strike
Against the wooden plank bed anymore.
I worked the midnight shift at a post office to send you dollars,
Bars of soap,
White laces,
Bottles of green oil.

I did not send you medicine,
But prayers. Every night, I prayed for you,
While I listened to the echo of your constant coughing,
Of the hard thumps against your aching body.

The day I heard you died, I looked at my face,
Half belonged to my mother,
Half to an unknown man,
And I cried with a fist, yours,
In my mouth.

FATHER

Are you the bald man
in that black-and-white photograph
Mother barred from me with her fingers?
And the 5×7 frame
and the black bordered pair of glasses
shoved me further into
a cell with no eye.

Are you the silent one
waiting for me outside the school wall
to raise me high to windless noon
to walk me halfway home with your tears?
Those dark drops I licked
and the saltiness on my tongue I preserved
until you told me ten years later
I was not your daughter.

You are without a daughter, and
I spit out the salt on my tongue.

I walk away from the history I made up,
from the land that was never mine.

CITIES AND A HISTORY

You walk into a city, and you see dull masks.
Children,
Young adults,
The elderly,
And the trees
Differ only in the number of creases.

All is still.

You reach out to touch the little child sitting on the hot pavement.
Her eyes are like dirty windows in winter, and mucus streams down
From her flat nose onto her bare hand.
"Poor child," you cry.
"Where are your parents?
Where is your home?"

The child does not speak. Her dark eyes lead you down a muddy path,
Where you see an empty house at the end—
No father,
No mother,
No food,
And no light.

There, you see you have neither history nor land
To claim your own.

There, you realize that after having walked the many cities and
    continents,
Only this city is real.
This city takes you back
To the place you never existed.

LOVERS

It's this body you see
Half-moons curve the waist,
Dark hair enshrouds the back
Like weeping willow branches swaying in the wind.

It's this body you feel
Flaring heat from solid calves, lean thighs.

It's this body you meddle with,
Not noticing the salty teardrops
Oozing from each pore.

WAR CHILDREN

Nineteen sixty-eight. Bombs churned the soil
Inside out.
Bodies flailed
Into the burning air.
Living people crawled and ran

Under secret tunnels.
My mother was in one of these tunnels,
Carried away hurriedly in a hammock by two farmers.
She was in labor.

In the midst of my mother's screams and other sounds,
I came to life, bloody and mute.
My grandmother slapped my buttocks to make me cry.
Thus, my life
Officially
Began.

My name is Huỳnh Thị Ngọc Hương. My brother is Huỳnh Công
   Sơn. We had different fathers, and Huỳnh was not the last name of
   either father. Huỳnh was the last name of a Vietnamese man whom
   my mother was in love with, but was never married to.

I do not know who my father is.

Once when I was nine,
I saw my mother showing her friend a photograph,
And I asked her,
Please, let me take a look at it.
The man in the photograph had a big nose, bald,
Wearing glasses with black rims.
Is he my father? I asked.
My mother took the photograph from my hand and told me
To go play outside.
I never asked her about my father again.

Besides the fact that I am 5´6˝ and that I have red-tinted hair,
I look Vietnamese.
My brother, on the other hand, would not be recognized
As Asian by anyone's standards.

When he was a child, his hair was blond—
Sun rays often bounced shadows on it.
His skin color was fairer than those around him.
I used to drape an embroidered white tablecloth over him
And carry him everywhere
On my back.
To me,
My brother was most beautiful.

To other children, he was the target of scrutiny.
They referred to him not by his name,
But as "Mỹ Tây Lai," (mixed American blood).
When he walked by, they yelled out verses:

Mỹ Tây Lai (mixed American blood)
Mười hai lỗ đít (with twelve butt holes)

Cái bụng con nít (with a child's stomach)
Cái đít chù vù (gigantic butt)
Con cu nhỏ xíu (tiny penis).

Some children threw pebbles at my brother.
Some shooed him as he came close to them.
Still, he wanted to be a part of their games.
Sometimes they'd let him, especially when they played war,
And he was assigned to be the red-skin Indian or the white-skin
    American.
My brother was thrilled, even though he knew that he had to die
At some point in the game.
The good guy could get shot and live to win the game,
But the bad guy must not argue about his death.

Day after day, my brother ran home crying,
Most of the time with bruises,

Cuts,
Or a bloody nose,
Or all of the above.
Anger soaked me thoroughly.
I slapped my brother on his face.
Why do you keep playing with those dogs?
Do you learn your lesson now?
My brother cried louder.

Where are they? I asked him.
He pointed his finger in their direction and led the way.
Those children met me with contemptuous looks.
They shamed me with their words.
My feet turned heavy. My tongue went numb.
I could not say anything worth saying.
Sometimes I cried.
I pulled my brother home by the hand.
I washed off his tears,
Nostrils,
And the dark streaks on his face.
I washed those bloody places on his fragile body,
Knowing that it would happen all over again.

When my brother was ten,
He became taller than most children in the neighborhood.
He could provoke fights.
He came home with more severe bruises and cuts,
But he cried less.

When the United States government passed a law
To sponsor its Amerasian children,
My mother immediately applied for our visas.
She was obsessed with the idea of going to America;
All her talks and future plans evolved around this dream.

During this time, there were many people escaping the country by
  boats.
My mother was anxious to leave Vietnam, and she considered this
  option.
However, she was hoping that our American heritage could earn us
Three plane tickets
And a safe arrival.

On one summer day in 1980,
My mother went to the market for her usual business.
This time, however,
She never came back.
We became orphans.
I was twelve years old,
My brother was eight.

THOSE DAYS

When your thumb and index finger clawed
The flesh of my thighs,
While you cried: "Stupid," "Stubborn!"
When your heels knocked my shins
Until I was down on the cement floor,
And you screamed: "Your face is a sign of doom,"
"Your face is a sign of damnation."
When your feet stamped my legs,
My waist, my rib cage,
And you howled: "Get away from me,
Save me from killing you!"

Did you know, Mother,
You would not live to see
This flesh you brought to life
Grown to a young woman
With your sad eyes
Your large nostrils
Your heart-shaped lips?

MOTHER

You locked me in your house.
Many nights I sat
On the cold tiled floor.
Through the door's thick glass,
I saw childrens' shadows.
I listened to their cries.
Laughter bit my ears.

Shadows were behind me, too.
Not of humans though.
There, on the walls,
Under the tables,
Behind doors,
By the gas stove,
Upstairs.

My body curled up.
Only two eyes remained
On the thick glass door
To search for you.

THE LAST DAY OF SAIGON

In my dream,
Fire and axes race behind us.
We tumble along dirt roads.
We crawl through tunnels.

I listen to Phantoms tear the sky.
I smell pungent from the war.
You are four years old again.
I am eight, your sister,
Whose fingers clamp your mouth.
To conceal your condemned American blood,
I sacrifice this body to the marching boots.

Don't leave me.
Don't.

In the night I curl like a shrimp
And dream of my intimate death.
In the day I think of your death,
In a motorcycle accident,
At a gathering, in the hands
Of strangers.

Let me weave my hands
Through your soft blond hair, as I used to.
Let me sing you a lullaby.

In your sleep,
I'll devour you.

TRAPPED THINGS

He wants a cigarette. The television is gone, there is no radio, and the
black leather jacket is in the pawn shop for forty dollars. He gets
out his penny jar and counts one hundred and six pennies. He puts
these pennies in a plastic bag and walks to the Circle K.

The cashier makes waves with her eyebrows. Her lips edge beautifully
as she says to him: "It's against our policy to accept only pennies."
He insists on counting them for her. He gets out the pennies and
starts to make a pile of ten. "I'm sorry, but it's against our policy,"
the cashier repeats.

His hands tremble.

These two hands!
These two hands lay still when they were struck with a large
wooden ruler
by his reading teacher.
These two hands stroked his sister's hair and wiped away her tears.
These two hands lifted lounge chairs and chlorine sacks day after day.

Now they tremble like orange leaves on the ground as he gathers the
pennies on the counter and puts them back in the plastic bag. In
front of the Circle K, he throws the bag with one hundred and six
pennies into the air.

What will he do with his hands?

LETTER TO MY BROTHER

It was just the other day I spoon fed you,
Scrubbed your buttocks in the shower,
And walked you to your kindergarten class.
It was just the other day we walked two miles to visit Mother in Mạc
    Đĩnh Chi.
I carried you on my back.
When it was your turn, your scrawny body dragged my feet on the
    ground.

It was just the other day we told each other our made-up stories.
Lying face to face, you wiped my tears, and I, yours.

It was just the other day you ran home,
Crying because children in the village said to you:
"Mỹ lai, go home to your American father."
I went out there to scream at them.
Their long tongues choked me, and I ran home
To forbid you from playing with those children,
Only to realize it would happen again.

It was just the other day Grandma spit chewed betel juice on our hands,
So we would not miss her too much.
On the airplane, you slept with your head leaning on my shoulder.
I watched the peace on your face and pledged to myself
That I would take care of you until the day I die.
You were twelve, I was sixteen and a half,
And Grandma said that we were going to America for a better future.

It was just the other day our American foster mother told me
That you got in fights in school.
You said those junior high students said to you: "Communist, go home!"

I howled, "Kill them. Kill all of them. I will help you."
Our foster mother stood with her mouth open like a dead fish.

It was just the other day you told me even though your friends
Were drug addicts and alcoholics,
You needed them.
"How can I choose friends from a decent family, sister?" you asked me.
"I'm also fucked up."

It was just the other day you called me from a public phone,
Telling me through your tears over and over again you loved me,
And you wanted my forgiveness for the lies and the pain
You had been causing me.
You were drunk, and you missed me because you saw your friend's sister
There partying with all of you,
And I was not.

Now you decide to join the US Marines.
It was never my or Grandma's dream to see you in the military.
Is it not enough that we are excrements of the war?
At the same time, I realize this may be your only opportunity to get
    out of Phoenix,
Of going from one job to another,
Facing homelessness every time.
You cry, "I am so scared, sister.
I have signed my life away."

It was just the other day that you sent me a check
For a million dollars with a note saying:
"This is to spend, Sis. When I win the lottery, I will send you
To the best medical school in the country—anywhere you want.
P.S. Would you send me $50 to buy some groceries?
With love. Your brother."

Now you are telling me that if you die
From a natural cause or on the line of duty,
I will receive one hundred thousand dollars.
Do not speak.
I do not want your death money.
I will burn it, and the smoke will pierce my eyes.

Allow me to stand silently in your arms.
In a while, you will kiss the top of my head
And ask me
Not to cry
When you turn to leave.

SIXTEEN HUNDRED DEGREES

Contained in a brown metal can,
Wrapped in a clear plastic bag,
Size like the tip of the index finger,
With perforations like a beehive,
They look like pieces of seashells.

"Those pieces," a man whispers,
"Are from a human's skeleton.
Cremated at sixteen hundred degrees,
Let cool, then ground."

I turn to look at the man,
Materials encasing his body turn
Ragged, white skin oozes yellow
Juice like eggnog. Suddenly, they dissipate,
All that remain as evidence of life are
Bones, once hard as tusks, now ground dust.

THE BODY

Here is the body of a young woman.
Here is a child trapped inside the body.
It watches the body make sex,
While it thinks of ways to escape.

WORDS AND CHILD

I did not want to go with you.
It would happen again,
You would take off my clothes, touch my body.
I stared at my sandals as you grabbed my hands.
I heard you say:
 "It's O.K.
 It's good for you.
 Do not tell your mother."

I did not want to go with you.
My breath jumped when you fingered my skirt.
The smooth floor—brother and I had
Gushed with water and slid on like trout—
Nipped my skin.

I sealed cries with palms over my cracked lips.
I buried my sandals and skirt under a mass of sand.
I pierced my eyes and eardrums with endless laughter.

But your words persisted.

AND THE STORY GOES

As I was told,
An arrogant elephant
Enjoyed stomping on
Little ants.

One day,
Ants climbed inside
Its ears
Bit its flesh, lightly.
The elephant groaned.
"Hit your head
On the stone,
The pain will stop,"
A quiet voice said.
So, the elephant hit
Its head
On the stone.
No pain!

Ants bit its flesh again.
"A little harder,"
Said the voice.
So, the elephant hit
Its head
On the stone
A little harder.
Harder.
Harder.
Its head cracked open.

And the story goes
I, too,

Pound my head
With the palms of
My hands
To soothe the head pain.

I lunge onto the floor,
All walls spin,
My head shrills,
Iron blade against a stone.
I hold my head,
Press it tight,
Pound it hard,
Pleading with the head pain,
Go away.

And I think
Of the arrogant elephant
As my pounding gets
Harder.

MANIFESTATIONS

A husband sketched a black Buddha
On his wife's left thigh
To keep her holy
While he was at war.

Upon his return, the husband found
Black Buddha, tired of sitting,
Had switched to her right thigh.

We, the women,
Whose fathers, uncles, and brothers
Shoveled our legs apart
Then engraved their manliness onto us,
We outline our Buddha
With bloody teeth.

And we lure our children
To sleep with love songs.

TOOLS AND HANDS

Give me a stone.
I will chisel it into a fine needle
That will mend the universe,
Its fragments of age and abuse.

These are tools handed to me:
    The basics: highlighters, syllabi, four-colored pens.
    A new identity: white coat, stethoscope, blue name tag.
    A new language: specificity, biopsychosocial, cyanotic, arthralgia.
    Knowledge of the body: kidney in cross section, brain in a bottle,
    Limbs in a black box, heart in a glass case.

I have come to know the length of the night.

Elaborate maps and pathways blur into strings of words and arrows,
While I dream of the poetry I have not yet written.

I am tattooed in my skin.

My hands are mangled.

Will it be worth the time I sit inside a room to
Memorize words, and stand
Outside myself to forget?

Am I the artist,
Or am I the stone?

I look into the eyes of an eighty-nine-year-old woman,
Whose loneliness is her disease.

She breaks her slice of bread into two halves,
Insisting that I eat one.

At Juvenile Hall, I meet boys
Who will not close their eyes.
So we imagine pleasant scenery with our eyes open.
These same eyes ignite when they ask me:

"Can a girl pee out semen after she has sex?"

"Why are my lips so pink?"

"If a hole is just a hole,
What is the big deal about rape?"

My ignorance lies elegantly
Beneath the white coat.

Tomorrow I will run through Golden Gate Park,
Eat flowers, smell the wet ground.
I acquire skills to be a physician,

But these hands will not be shaped
By the tools I must use.

These hands will write poetry,
Hold a dying woman,
Take a pulse.

LOST LOVE

Once a happy fool, now a sober poet—the weaver of words.
Words that howl confused senses of a lost love,
Ache like a mother's breasts, painful from the retention of her milk,
Since there is no longer her young
To suck on them.

OYSTERCATCHERS

Oystercatchers, running from the waves,
Running toward the waves.
Their legs are tilted twigs,
Stepping one in front of the other,
Two inches, then another two inches.
So quick, incredibly quick.

If I were to run, they would fly away.
If I were to walk, I would lose the race.

Oystercatchers, running away, toward, away, toward,
While the immense body of water boils,
Not from anger, most likely not,
But from eternal restlessness.

MEDICAL STUDENT'S CONTEMPLATION

It does not matter how big or small,
How tough or gentle,
How important or lowly
A man is.

Once dressed in a hospital gown,
His bare legs dangling from the gurney,
His hands holding onto his penis,

All the medical student sees are the rashes and bumps
On his fleshy scrotal sac.
And the doctor scrutinizes only unusual lesions or discharges
For evidence of STDs.

CHILD'S STEPS

He asked the bus driver
If the bus was the forty-four.
She must have said "Yes,"
As she revved the engine.
He paid with coins and staggered
Toward the front seats.
He smelled of liquor,
Sweat, cigarettes—
Recent odors mixed with old ones,
Like patches on a frayed shirt.

He sat down on a seat vacated
For seniors and disabled persons.
His eyes scanned the rows of faces.

I was sitting nearby,
Humming a made-up tune.
I smiled and nodded at him.

The man looked down at his hands.

He turned to face me again.
"You're beautiful," he said.
He smiled and suddenly looked young
For his peppered hair.

The bus pulled to a stop at
The corner of Ninth Street and Irving.
The man walked down the step slowly.
I watched his steps,
Those his mother once treasured.

OUR DANCE

The tear-drop shaped pumpkin seed is
Half an inch beneath the soil.
Over the course of one week, the soil pushes upward,
Forms a mound, expands all around,
Bursts and reveals the seed's pole.
Its tip cracks—
A lime green sprouts through.

The two leaves unfurl.
The pumpkin seed erupts in three days.

Such life!
Such daring desire!

CROWN OF A SMILE

There is a white mark on the back of a bird
That circles and flies away.
There is a boy who makes love to me
And falls in love with someone else.
There are feelings that I hide
Like seams in undergarments.

I wear the crown of a smile,
Fooling those who want to be fooled.
The fooler and the fools.

DREAMS

These days I dream of newborns
Left in a corner of an empty hut,
On a table in the midst of a festival.
I do not know if those children are mine.
I have lost my mind!
Frantically I write down segments of my life—
Told by a woman—

These days my limbs guide me near the waters.
The sky is gray.
Still, the waves are grayer.
I see stick figures through the mist.
Forever claimed by the sea,
They walk without moving.
Something whispers:
"Walk straight. Walk straight."

My heart pulsates, but I am drawn to silence.

These days my body searches for your body,
Which is warm, wet, and full of motion.
My mouth opens to swallow you,
My language pleads for you to understand:
    That I am raped by a dry fecal stick;
    That I fear being forgotten
    Like rain curtains on a glass window;
    That I am fragrance pushing against the wind.
These days I no longer resent you for not seeing
The ghosts of my past—they entice me only.

Even though I want to look at
The sunflowers in your green eyes,
I let you sleep.
I turn to the ceiling.

YOU ASK

"What if tomorrow all the men in this world vanished?"

I will love women,
The humankind I am most familiar with.
This body was in Mother's arms the moment I first cried.
Grandmother fed me chewed rice from her mouth.
Auntie held me up as I took my first falling step.

"What if tomorrow all the men in this world became lost?"

I will return to the friend of my soul.
This teardrop we crack into two halves,

And laughter, we jostle in the open night.
We acknowledge the contours of our shared body.
We plan to become country doctors.
I, also a very part-time singer, and she, a dancer.

"What if tomorrow all the men turned their faces away?"

With heart crowned on my head,
I will walk on foot to an ocean of greens.
There will be calla lilies and sunflowers,
And birds rising where mothers and children play.

CHANTING

Nam mô a di đà bà gịa,
Đá tha già đá dạ, đa địa dạ tha,
A di ly đô bà tỳ, a di ly đa tất đam bà tỳ,
A di ly ca tì ca lan đế, a di ly đa tì ca lan đa,
Dà di nị dà dà na, chỉ đa ca lệ ta bà ha.

When I was twelve
I rode Grandmother to the temple
On the back of a purple bicycle.
I learned to pray, words
I realized eleven years later
I did not understand.

Nam mô a di đà bà gịa, đá tha già đá gịa, đa địa dạ tha

Someone hit my foster mom's head
While she was drunk,
Standing in a telephone booth.

She woke up in an open field
And remembered only the fingers
That pulled down the zipper.

A di ly đô bà tỳ, a di ly đa tất đam bà tỳ

This was my American mother
Who taught me to say:
"May I have a sheet of paper?"
Instead of saying: "May I have a shit of paper?"
Who became tongue-tied while trying to help me
Hear the difference
Between "beach" and "bitch."
Who held my hand
As we crossed the parking lot
To go to the grocery store.
She, twenty-nine, 5' 9", with a hip-length blond wig,
I, sixteen, 5' 6", with dark hair.

A di ly đô bà tỳ, a di ly đa tất đam bà tỳ,
A di ly ca tì ca lan đế, a di ly đa tì ca lan đa,
Dà di nị dà dà na, chỉ đa ca lệ ta bà ha

I now know more words than she does.
Yet I find none to soothe her pain.

So here, in the midst of burning incense and tears,
I return to Grandmother
And to this chant
I still do not understand.

I pray: Teach us to listen
Teach us to forgive our suffering
Teach us to understand others' suffering.

Nam mô A Di Đà Phật
Nam mô Đại Từ Đại Bi cứu khổ cứu nạn Quán Thế Âm Bồ Tát.

AN ANT

I hear a child crying
At her own made-up stories.
I see a young girl
Crawling under the bed to avoid
An engorged sex.
I smell the pile of trash
A woman is staring vacantly at,
While her breasts hang
Like eggplants in her infant's mouth.
I taste blood from an old woman's finger.
She is sewing a pocket into the underwear
Her granddaughter will be wearing
On her way to America.

These women have become me.

As if I were an ant,
Carrying a lump of sugar
Too heavy on my back,
I am tired. Tired.
I imagine a gigantic foot
Crushing life out of me.

There is lightness
In the dust
I return to.

SCENT

You ask if my childhood was magical.
Look at me: A lanky child,
Wandering through crowded streets of Saigon.
My sandals scraping rhythmic edges,
While I sang songs of my daily life.
I lost my virginity at age nine.
At ten, another man hovered on top of my body,
While my mother stood nearby,
Diplomatic and sweet-voiced:
"Let her go, older brother.
She's just a child."

Of all that is lost,
I hang on to the memory of a late
Afternoon. My mother did not
Visit home for five days, and
Grandma had just lost the last of our
Allowance to a local bet.
Dinner that night composed of a pot
Of steamed rice and soy sauce to dip
With *rau muống*, a kind of greens that
Grow easily in mud and ponds.

We sat down on the tiled floor
I had scrubbed earlier.

Grandma said to me:

"Con ơi, nghèo cho sạch.

Rách cho thơm."

My child, though you are poor,

Remember to stay clean.

Though you are torn,

Remember to maintain your scent.

Sitting with folded legs,

We inhaled the vapor of steamed rice.

REFUGEES

Dragging their dark

Bodies, thin as fibrous

Roots, wearied as torn

Leaves, under the blade of

The reaper, they search

For sanctuary.

SLEEP SHADE

The autumn sun rays illuminate half

The yellow rose, leaving the lower

Half in shadow. A spider web

Briefly becomes visible. A young

Woman looks out the window. Her body

Wants her to lie it down to rest.

IN TIME OF WAR

On a rainy day, a man
Once lay next to me in the half light,
As I listened to my body desiring.
Two women were conversing in
The alley below. Water bounced on
The tin roof. A fan was humming.
These sounds brought me back to

April days of 1975
My brother and I then children
Of a losing war, hiding among
Concrete walls and crippled soldiers.
Frightened by rumors that the
Communists would behead Amerasians,
I embraced my brother and left my
Childhood for the sounds of rain and electric fans.

In the half light,
I listened to my body's desire.
This man, too, was of mixed blood.
We clung to each other with no arms.

THIS RIVER

I feel a pang of emotion,
That which I hesitate to accept;
Yet I am unable to resist its irresistibility.
You and I exist together,
Under the moon and amidst the sounds:
Music, twirling of human energy.

I could have forgotten your name.

Your face might have blurred amongst thousands.

But your touch would always remain—the touch

That soothed my soul,

While it set my spirit afire.

You amaze me with your naked curiosity, your daring passion.

To you, I am River. And the river in me springs forth.

This River

Contains rotting flesh and feces discarded.

This River

Nurtures life and growth,

And loves it all the same—

The fish and the floating algae always carry on their separate journeys.

This River

Drowns tears and mute yearnings.

This River

Modulates in the sunlight,

Stretches silk,

Breathes the fragrance of desires.

Immersed in my waters, we surge forth as evening tides.

Our present moment inspires the contour. And tomorrow?

    Forever a part of the river's course.

MUSTARD GREENS

My lunch today, stir-fried

Bitter green leaves with

Soy sauce, a pinch of sugar,

And leftover rice. The bitter

Leaves my mother used to
Cook often because I did
Not like them, making me
Sit at that table until I
Finished every leaf. Food turned
Watery in my mouth as I dreamed
Of my death, of her death.

The bitterness of Khổ Qua,
Also green, stuffed with
Tofu and peanuts, swollen
Like the penis my uncle
Placed on my hand.
How many times at age nine?

The bitter medicine an
Old Chinese man gave
Me for my white discharge,
Asking me if I had ever
Been "close" to a man.
And I, at age fifteen,
Knowing better than to
Disrespect an elder,
Screamed at him anyway,
Ran out the door and
Tripped over what had been
Blocked out of my
Mind since age nine—
The coarse cement floor,
The drooling penis,
The words, words, words,

His words, her words, my
Words, trying to explain,

Trying to understand, trying
To forgive. Why? I asked.
He, who was young, handsome,
Playing the guitar and singing
Cải Lương into the night.
Why did he take what's mine?

He, now in his fifties, scrawny,
Already lost bladder control,
Kneeling across me, sobbing:
"I don't know why."

And she, dead, unable
To answer my questions, leaving
Me to crave these bitter
Leaves, to buy them, cook, and
Eat them by myself.

THE TWO WOMEN

Soon I will be older than my mother,
Knowing her more through my own
Aging features, these sad eyes,
This broad-based nose, cleaved
At the tip, these heart-shaped lips,
Pressed hard during outbursts
Of anger, she, pinching my thighs
With her thumb and index
Finger, aiming clay bowls at my body;

I sit stone-faced,
Unable to look at my best friend or my lover—

My objects of anger—wishing to
Never see them again. Wanting
To hurt them, frightened by
My own malice, by the white
Wall surging in my chest.

Afterwards, I sit on the tiled floor,
She quietly rubs Tiger Balm on my bruises;
I embrace myself,
Like an infant wrapped in my dead
Mother's blouse, sniffing
The familiar scent.

THIS PATH

You ran through tunnels beside
The makeshift stretcher that carried my mother,
Who was still bleeding, and me, a newborn,
Mute in blotched rags, while
American bombers shredded
Your home and village above.

Begging for our refuge, you were
Shooed away for bringing bad karma—
Mother and child out of wedlock.
Yet, you marked me the daughter of
Buddha—born with three
Hair clumps on my head as if
Shaved by a monk.

With no preaching, you led me
To temples, holding my hand as

We took the rickshaw, clutching
My waist as I grew older and rode
You on the back of the purple bicycle.

Signing your name with an "X,"
You hired an English tutor for me,
Asking me to speak foreign
Words, repeating "Dooo" for dog,
"Ka-to" for cat, laughing
Like an excited child.
You recited by memory the epic
Poem "Truyện Kiều," the story of
Kiều, a young woman whose talent and
Fate condemned each other. It was your
Story, too, a beauty of your village,
A gifted riddle inventor, wishing to be a
Nun, instead, married off to a stranger,
Who wrapped your hair around
His forearm like a garment and
Yanked it from the scalp.

You counted the black rosary beads
And advised me to go to America.
Your only request: that I raise my brother,
Obtain a higher education
Then become a nun.

Grandmother, did you always know
This is the path of my life?
Help me to understand it.
Help me to accept it.
I have ventured exciting and tired steps,
Now returning.

HÒ

I eat a tomato a day—
Oatmeal tomato soup,
Zucchini tomato soup,
Stir-fry with tomatoes,
Tomato salad. . . .

"Tomatoes are good for your skin,"
Grandma used to tell me.

My mother disappeared
When I was twelve.
One by one, Grandma sold my mother's
Gold bars, bracelets, rings to
Raise my brother and me.

She would buy a tomato
And a bundle of bitter leaves.
Squatting by the water faucet
In the kitchen, she washed them
And gave them to me in a bowl.
"Eat. Eat," Grandma told me.
"Tomatoes are good for your skin."

Lying on a straw mat at night,
Grandma told me stories of her
Girlhood, stuffing pillows under
Blankets, sneaking out of the house
To sing riddles, "*hò*," with other girls and boys.
Once I asked Grandma to "*hò*" for me.
She laughed and turned tomato cheeks.
"I'm too old," she said.

I rubbed Grandma's aching body.
When she fell asleep,
    I made up "hò" under my breath:

Hò ơ,
Trời mưa bong bóng bập bồng.
Mẹ đi lấy chồng,
Con ở với ai?

Hò ơ,
The rain rains bubbles, bobbing.
Mother left to remarry,
The child lives with whom?

Hò ơ,
Trời mưa bong bóng bập bồng.
Mẹ đi lấy chồng,
Con ở với Ngoại.

Hò ơ,
The rain rains bubbles, bobbing.
Mother left to remarry,
I live with Grandma.

SCENT OF NAKEDNESS

I have seen an operated heart.
Small heart like a plum split open.
No fat around it yet to mark the passing years. Blue draping and
    colored tubes, woven into its blood vessels like the medusa.
Will I remember the child lying beneath it all?

My heart is the stem of the aspen leaf, and love is the leaf. Shall I choose the man who is in my blood? Or shall I choose the man who persists?

Will inertia keep me bloated? Will someone care enough to step on my abdomen to deflate the pain?

Shall I continue to walk through the tunnel of my past?
    Will I spend the rest of my
life writing about these years?
Will my uncle stop molesting me, as he has stopped smoking in
    order to breathe?
Will I become the woman I have wanted?
I will not make up a name to address these questions, will not
    feed the illusion of knowing the unknowable.
An answer is like the ending of a poem—it discovers me.

SẦU RIÊNG (DURIAN)

Ai mua trăng? Tôi bán trăng cho.
Chẳng bán chuyện buồn đau,
Của riêng mình.

Who wants to buy the moon? She
Will sell you the moon,
But private sadness—it is hers.

The fruit is *sầu riêng*.
Oval shaped and big as a melon,
It has a wood-like rind.
Its self-defense: five-
Centimeter-long, broad-based needles.

She carries private sadness
At the thumb-thick stub.

She pries it open with a
Thick, sharp knife—

Four separate chambers,
Each holding three flesh-
Dipped seeds,
Size of limes, color of lemons.
The flesh is soft and silky.
The seed is brown.

There are those who think it smells
Like sewage, but she
Loves private sadness—
Its exquisite, sharp, late summer
Night fragrance.

She boils the seed
And eats it, too.
Its taste, the warmth of armpit
And baby's breath.

SONGS OF A QUIET WARRIOR

1.
She left the rice fields,
Her ancestral altar,
Her mother and four siblings
To go to Saigon city.

Her dream at fifteen:
To strive beyond the ordinary.

Perhaps it was her first
Time taking the train, going further
Than the diameter of her village,
Then made into a maid.
The oldest son wanted to teach
Her more words, but the youngest
Girl with the yellow hair ribbon
Trashed her notebook, broke
Her pencil—the hairline of jealousy
Rose to more cruel mischief.

In her mother's dream, she came home,
Crying the girl's name:
"*Con Tí, con Tí.*"
Her mother sold baskets of rice
For a train ticket,
Finding her silent
Mouth at the doorstep.
"Ask your mother to come in,"
The man of the house said.
"Get her water.
Cut the pig open," he added.

Thongs in one hand, her mother
Scribbled the air with the other,
Saying: "No, no. Don't cut the
Pig open. I'll eat only vegetables this month."

She came back with the water,
And a broken clay pig.
She had been saving money,

By using less soap when she washed
People's clothes, by not
Buying sweets for herself.

2.

The day I last saw my mother,
She had on a pair of black pants
And a coffee colored *áo bà ba*—
A long-sleeved nylon shirt,
Buttoned in the middle,
Split down from the waist line
On both sides, embroidered
Around the neck and the hems.

I stood on the stairway and watched her
Giving Grandma money for the day's
Groceries, before she went to visit
My rich dad, who came to look
For her three days later.

Then the news, a naked body found
Floating in the river
In a plastic bag, her arms tied
To her bent legs.
Grandma told me to pray it was
Not my mother's body.

The morning Grandma, my aunt,
And my rich dad went to the morgue,
I sat on the toilet, cemented with
One thought. *I was free!*
Free of my mother, her
Beatings, her shouts.

3.

My mother was a prostitute.
I saw pictures of her sitting at
An office desk in a Vietnamese
Traditional dress *áo dài*.
But I knew she was a prostitute.
No war promotes honest living.

I cannot recall who told me,
Not likely my mother, that I
Might have had an older sibling.
She must have aborted him.
My younger brother was blond
With beautiful white skin.

I loved him, although he looked
Nothing like me. To this day,
I still try to find the resemblance
Between us. I say to him:
"We have the exact same hands!"
"We have similar mannerisms."
He laughs every time.
"I love you, Sister," he says.
"It's okay that I am more beautiful."

4.

Once I saw my mother sleeping naked,
Her legs kicked open,
The mound of her pubis wide
Like an intelligent forehead.
I had seen her through the keyhole
In the act of tired sex many times.

But that morning, my mother was sleeping.
Her body was at one with her desire.

I wanted to look at her sad eyes,
Which have become my sad eyes.
I wanted to kiss her heart-shaped lips,
Which have become my lips.
I wanted to touch the mound of her pubis,
Which has become my mound.

I watched her sleep instead.

DAYS OF APRIL

(In memory of Mr. Arthur Lee Williams)

This coffin is not home,
No more than the hospital bed,
Where we shook hands, latched
Fingers, stacked fists.
Where I found you fastened
To the chair, head drooped
Sideways, pleading:
"Take these straps off me, Moon.
Let me go home and do
What you're doing here for me."

Everyone wrote orders—
The pain team, my medicine team,
Your private doctor.
Each day you said: "It hurts."

Your "hurts" sounded like "hearts."
I rubbed Icy Hot on your left
Shoulder, your right hip.
My thumb on your cancerous
Bones—a probing lullaby.

Dysarthria, dysphasia—
Your mouth a stagnant, tilted
Pond after the stroke.
The "B.M. Queen" I was, checking
Daily records of your bowel movements.
    Discontinue colace please.
    Enema now.
Eagerly, I wrote these orders.

What else could a medical student do?

Those were sunny days of April.
I watched you drown in morphine dreams,
Calling me "Mum," whispering you loved me.
Your belly changed from distended
To flattened to concave.

    The patient does not wish for tube feeding.
    The patient does not wish for IV hydration.
    The patient wishes to go home.
    No code.

I wrote it again and again
In my progress notes,
Like a prisoner searching
For the button I tossed in my dark cell—
A game to keep myself sane.

I touch death in your hands,
Strangely cold and properly rested
On your abdomen.
I cry and my tears are not chains,
But a white butterfly's wings.

LETTING GO

Torn blue underwear, written messages,
Letters, pictures, journals. . . .
I brought them from Tempe
To Tucson to San Francisco like
A turtle carrying its house.
Each memory ripples concentric memories.
I am the past.

Tear messages, letters, and pictures.
Throw away the pair of underwear.
These hands tremble as they destroy.
Tearing faster, skimming through
The years of yearning. A girl,
Who loved boys and feared older men.

These hands tremble as they let go.

A FOREIGNER

This is home,
The same tiled floor

I used to sleep on, after lunch.
The dresser limps with the added ten years,
The bed is still in the exact corner,
And my mother's portraits smile down
From the walls.

This is the home
My mother bought with her sweat
Of a maid and her flesh of a prostitute.
So that her mother, sister, brother,
Children may live under the same roof.

From the balcony, I see girls
Of my age grown pregnant
With household responsibilities.
The street vendor's back
Now hunches near to the ground.
I am home, yet my tongue
Speaks awkwardly my mother's language.
My digestive system violently
Churns her food.

This is home, memory sings.

GRANDMOTHER'S TOMB

The epitaph of Jalaludin Rumi read: "When we are dead, seek not our
   tomb in the earth, but find it in the hearts of men."

   Where is your tomb?

Gone now. A cemetery reconstructed
Into a playground.
The dead upturned.

"I don't want to be cremated,"
You once said.
"It's too hot."

I knelt by the oven, listening
To the dancing crackles of firewood.
In the field, my uncle and cousins
Chased after grasshoppers.
Their bodies curved like flames.

I sprinkled your ashes with green
Oil, your favorite for colds and aches.
Once, having broken the bottle of green
Oil, you saved the soaked towel under
Your pillow to sniff every night,
While my young hands milked your
Wrinkle-bound flesh and
Pressed on your small bones.

The strength in my hands comes
From these years.
Grandmother, the other day a friend
Said I had your eyes.
In the mirror, my mother's sad
Eyes had evolved into a gentle, deep gaze,
Your high cheekbones raised my smile.

IMPERMANENCE

Suppose my love is the wave revisiting the shore.
Why do we want so much to hold on,
Knowing each passionate embrace has its inevitable departure?

MY KINDRED

For John Seaver (January 26, 1965–September 25, 1999)

My kindred, spirit-man,
I have come to this shore to be with you,
As I have done innumerable times in my lives.
And when I found you,
When we found one another,
Our hearts knew unspeakable knowledge,
Our spirits recognized shared ancient times.

My kindred, spirit-man,
The ocean before me is immense,
And I am small, utterly small.
What do I know of fate?
I know nothing.

Yet I feel you out there,
In the waves,
Within those winged birds,
Between clouds and sunrays.

Everywhere I look, your eyes look.

My kindred, spirit-man,
I have come to this shore to offer you

A prayer and a wish;
  To be at one with the energy
  You have immersed yourself in;
  know you,
  Once again.

SPIRIT PATH

If you have loved someone,
If you have cared for another,
If you have wiped away tears,
If you have shared laughter,
Then you have lived,
You have lived your human heart.

And your love will always be here
To comfort her through lonely times,
To lift her up for she knows she's loved,
To help her flower,
To strengthen her faith.

If you have loved someone,
If you have cared for another,
If you have wiped away tears,
If you have shared laughter,
Then you have set,
You have set her free.

And your love will always be here
To show the beauty in her every day,
To help her seek her true destiny,

To grace her with peace,
To guide her home.

If you have loved someone,
Then you have walked,
You have walked a spirit path.

TORCHBEARERS

1.
My aunt's letter arrived today,
Four pages of onionskin paper
To minimize the postage, costing
More than she made in a week,
Selling cigarettes on the street
From noon until two in the morning.

She wrote,
"My stomach turns feverish,
Hearing you're exhausted
From the hospital work.
Why would you stand so long
That your legs wobbled, your hands
Cramped on the retractor? And why
Chest pain in a girl your age?
Educated people eat a pig's brain
Each day to nurture their health.
You are alone and far away,
But you don't love your own body.
I wish I could be there to
Cook for you."

In blue ink, she went on:
"Our ancestors have a saying:
'Unhurriedly pick falling flowers.
Such determination is better
Than natural talent.'
Take time to rest.
It's fine whenever you graduate."

This same woman had insisted I quit
High school to sell sweets and cigarettes.
Poverty made her a jealous stepmother.
Grandma would sit on the plank bed
And spit betel juice into a metal can.
Grandma, who only knew to sign
Her name with an "X,"
Sent my brother and me to America,
Saying even if we had to eat dirt,
It would be less humiliating there.

It's been twelve years since the day
Grandma watched us walk away with
A brown handbag. A woman in
The United States, still I wipe tears
And snot on the cuff
Of my pants the way Grandma,
Auntie, and Mother did on theirs.

2.
My aunt's letter arrived today.
"Such a trial to be a woman, oh my child."
Childless, she was forced to leave
Her first husband. Her second man
Left her for his old sweetheart, although
She bore him a son. She married

The third time to a widower,
Whose ten children became hers to raise.

"Your mother couldn't endure your stepfather,"
She went on.
"He was too strong.
She had to hide from him,
Causing many arguments between them.
You were too young to understand."

Children then, my brother and I,
Walking three kilometers to see
Our mother, excited to each get
One *đồng* from our rich dad—
Six years younger than Grandma.
He asked us to play outside for an hour,
Even though we had just arrived.

My aunt added,
"Grandma used to say:
'The cock harms the hen.'
Strong men cause women to
Waste away. Then all sorts of illness,
Poor vision, ear ringing, weak limbs.
One hundred kinds of poison, none equal
To the root of the man.
Grandma said this often when
She was still alive. I think it's very true,
Very logical."

Wishing to be a nun, instead
Grandma was married off to a stranger,
Who brought women to his front porch
While Grandma cooked and washed in the back.

"Grandma didn't care to get jealous.
She stayed inside and slept soundly.
That was why she looked rosy and healthy
In old age. If her husband had
Always been around like a rooster,
She might have died young."

No mention in the letter that Grandma
Had begged her mother to let her come home.
The old woman cried, as she sent her child
Back, saying: "A young woman is destined
To the twelve waters,
Rejoice if it's clear,
Endure if it's muddy."

These torchbearers
Their legacies
Bless me and haunt me.
Will I suffer their same fates?
Will I be able to liberate
Them in me?

OLD VOW

As I am about to embark upon this next journey,
I pray that I remain humble and loving;
That I am true to those I love and care for;
That I work hard and feel at peace at the end of the day;
That I am attentive to my physical and emotional health;
That I continue to grow spiritually deep and wise.

And if I were to die in the midst of a day,
I wish to be ready.

CLOCKWISE
FROM TOP

Sister Dang
Nghiem's
grandmother
in the
early 1960s.

Sister Dang Nghiem
(age six)
and brother,
Sonny Huynh
(age two) in 1974.

Sister Dang Nghiem
in 1970 (age two).

Mother (age twenty-four), grandmother (age fifty-eight), and
Sister Dang Nghiem (baby Huong Huynh) in 1968.

Sister Dang Nghiem at her graduation from the University of Arizona in 1993.

Poetry recitation in San Francisco (1996).

John Seaver in 1998.

Nirmala Convent & Hospital in Bihar, India (1996).

Sister Dang Nghiem and her brother, Sonny, at Sister D's graduation from the UCSF School of Medicine (1999).

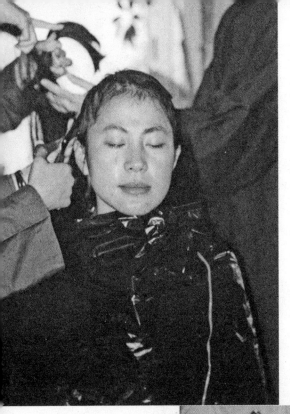

CLOCKWISE FROM LEFT

Sister D's novice
ordination ceremony
on May 18, 2000.

"Shedding my hair completely,
I vow to transform all my
afflictions."

Sister D, pictured with Thầy,
as a new novice immediately
after ordination.

PART 2.

FEATHER ON
A MIDDAY

Poems after
Monastic Ordination
(2000–present)

WHAT DOES A NUN DO ALL DAY?

All day long, I have only myself to be with,
Coming back to be aware of
Each step I take,
Each breath I inhale,
Each thought passing by.

All day long, I have only myself to look at,
When the wall of anger rises,
When hurt fills my chest,
When tears are shedding,
I tell myself, it's okay, it's okay.
I am here.

All day long, I have only my
"Self" to let go.

AS IT IS

I can be engrossed
In learning French, reading sutras,
But this heavy feeling inside me is still there.

Wherever I go, there it is.
Whatever I do, there it is.

This IT gnaws at me.

I wish to lie down and expire,
But IT will not deteriorate with my body,
Just as a tree may collapse,

But from its roots, it is continued.

One day, then another passes by,
I'm growing older.
I feel my aging, in the achiness of this body,
The sensitivity of the digestive tract,
The coldness of these extremities.

What have I done
To become freer?

I gave up a doctor's fame.
I shaved my head and look
Like somebody I myself don't recognize.
I keep three sets of clothes
And would be happy to give up
This heavy IT
Along with my extra robes to Sister Abbess.
Yet, I know IT is mine to sit with,
To embrace, to understand, and to transform.

IT is my daily death and sustenance.
IT is my one-way ticket to liberation.

FREEDOM

My love came to me by train to
Reconfirm his loyalty.
My lips were still the color crimson, but
I touched my shaven head and
Vowed to honor his freedom,
So that we may forever be one.

PURPLE FLOWER ON THE SIDE ROAD

On a sunny autumn day, I thought you had gone.
In the dark night that followed, I howled your name
As the ocean raged menacing waves.
Alone, so small.
I prayed for your protection, my love.

Where did you go? Can my piercing cries find you?
At the bottom of the cliff, my body in pieces?
Your portrait stares silently.
In despair, there is only "I" and cruel loss.

Because there is still "I," there is still "you," still union and separation.
The breath whispers non-death.
Is it not true that we have never been strangers?

When our eyes were still too shy to look at one other,
Our minds were already deeply connected.
Now your hands continue to embrace me,
The purple flower on the side of the road, a shared smile.

In one instant, you left.
In one mindful moment, you are all that is.

DIALOGUE WITH THE GRASPING MIND

Hello there, my grasping mind!
We have been together forever.
Yet, each time you appear,
As if for the first time
I encounter your luring abyss.

Melancholy fills up my chest.
Restlessness makes me want to howl
And beat your heaviness into
Dust.

Dear one, I will run no more.
Tell me about the things you grasp.
Is it this body, young and supple?
The silky skin left uncaressed?

You ask, why me?
Thirty-three years old, why must I be
Forgotten in oversized brown robes?

Or is it you, grasping mind, who grasp
The object you yourself have created?
What needs do you fulfill?

This body has welcomed comforts,
Exalted in pleasures, lain with
Loneliness, numbed by despair.
This body crashes suddenly,
Without the strength to drag itself to
The bathroom. Every muscle aches.
The mid-night chest pain is suffocating.
The abdominal bloating,
The bleeding anus,
The ulcerous mouth,
The gnawed fingers. . . .

I know of many ways to kill myself,
But I cannot stifle my sadness.
I cannot outrun my own grasping.

Here, I stand still
To embrace you, so there is a chance
For true love.

BEGINNING ANEW

Last night in my dream,
I realized that I had been unskilful.
While looking for you to begin anew with,
I learned that you had died!

This morning in sitting meditation,
I embraced my feelings of regret.
Taking refuge in my light breath,
I consoled myself:
You never held anything against me.

Thank you, dear one,
For accepting all that I am,
So that I may face my shame.

Thank you, dear one,
For loving me unconditionally,
So that I may transform and blossom.

EMBRACING THE WOUNDED CHILD

Mother is a five-year-old child,
Running happily in the rain.

Father is a gaunt boy,
Digging his hands deep in the sand.

I sit still in meditation,
Smiling tenderly.

SEARCHING FOR THE ONE

I search for the one who loves me in my every step, every breath.
I search for the one whom I love in the thousand paths coming home.

MAN IN A CAVE

Man in a cave, only knows of darkness.
If there is one day,
Sunlight shines through a crevice.
Would you believe,
Would you believe,
The distance between darkness and the sun
Is a block of stone?

COMING HOME

Buddha is my breath,
Giving me life in this moment and
Acceptance of what was, is, and will be.

Buddha is right view:
Ego is the root
Of my afflictions.

Buddha is my shame,
Helping me to stop and
Recognize my unskillfulness.

Buddha is this lotus posture,
Stable and light.
Breath, body, and mind unify.

The work worth doing
Is now.

EMBRACE

I come to myself and I say:
I am here for you, little sister.
For the swollen slashes on your wrists and
Forearms, translucent like leeches
Gasping under the strokes of my hands
Some resemble fibrous stumps.

I am here for you, little sister.
Breathing in, I feel the heaviness in my chest.
Breathing out, my abdomen is engorged with pain.
Seventeen years old, you are,
What have you gone through?

I had lost both parents.
I had endured curses and beatings.
I had been molested.
I had gone to rivers for comforts
In imagined deaths.
I had left Vietnam—
My inheritance: a young brother,
Grandmother's hopes, and a muted child within.

I am here for you, dear one.
The bell for dinner resounds with insistence.
Breathing in, I know I am breathing in.
My cravings suffocate me.
I want to leave this sitting cushion.
I want to go to the dining hall.
I want to eat.
Breathing out, I know I am breathing out.
I am aware that my mind wants to take refuge in food.
The solace of flavor
Will end at the throat,
But the abdominal bloating and self-defeat
Will carry on into the night,

As they have over the years, years of eating
Pound cakes and sipping beers in front of the television.
I would leave restaurants, only to return
To order a second meal to-go.
One Valentine's night, I finished two pounds
Of cookies, alone on my bunk bed.

When sadness and restlessness were overwhelming,
I turned to food.

I am here for you, following my breathing.
Twenty minutes into dinner time, and
The cravings have subsided.
My in-breath is quieter,
My out-breath is deeper.
Breathing in, I am aware of my body.
The space in my chest is more open.
Breathing out, I bring peace to my body.
There is lightness in my abdomen.

Breathing in, I feel gladness,
To have sat here for you, whose slashes
Sag like stretch marks on an old woman's belly.
For the muted child,
Who could not escape from the strip.
For the young woman,
Who assumed the abuser's role.
Breathing out, I feel gratitude,
For the Buddha, my Teacher, my Sisters.
For this space and time to stop.
For the energy and the strength to stop.
I have stopped for one hour!

Breathing in, I am aware of my mind.
Faith in the Dharma strengthens.
Breathing out, I liberate my mind.
Quietude imbues me.

Breathing in, I contemplate impermanence.
My cravings have subsided,
And your slashes, too, will return to the earth.
Breathing out, I see that even your suffering,
However familiar and poignant it may be,

Is not for me to hoard or to become.
Breathing in, I see no-birth and no-death.
You and I are cuts of the same fabric.
Breathing out, I heal you,
Fractal inside of me.

Breathing in, I practice letting go.
·Breathing out, I am home.

OAKS IN WINTER

I am learning
To be like the oaks standing
Still
While snowflakes
Gush
Miniature waterfalls

The branches stay
Still,
Their autumn leaves stay
Still—
Not even
One
Perceptible movement—

Holding
Quietly
The buds
Inward.

ON THE EIGHTH DAY OF FASTING AND NOBLE SILENCE

Birds are singing outside the window.
Sun beams penetrate amidst thunder.
I sit, holding a bowl of warm water,
In quietude, without wishes, without prayers.

INNER EYES

I saw myself
Sitting at a vendor
With my mother and brother
Eating sweet soup or
Perhaps a salty dish—
The first and only time
Mother rewarded my good grades.
How special I felt!

I saw Grandma
Sitting on the plank bed
Quietly sewing a small pocket onto
My mother's black underwear.
I was to wear them to America
With a five-dollar bill in the pocket.
The next day
Grandma rubbed chewed betel nut
On my palms to help me
Not to miss her too much.
Aware that I'd never again see Grandma
I clutched my brother's hand,

Walking into the drizzling
Rain mixed with tears.

I saw myself
Sitting alone at a desk on late nights
A college student, red-eyed,
Weary, raw energy pushing,
Scrambling for
A place in the world.

I saw myself
Mesmerized by the mountain range—
"Purple mountains," John said softly.
I could feel the desert breathing,
Mountains stretching,
Quiet peace flowing through my partner.

I saw myself
Watching autumn leaves with him.
Some twirled
Some spiraled
Some zigzagged
Some held stillness in their movements
Some zipped straight to the ground.
Dancers they were,
Proceeding with their own dances
As they all returned
To Mother Earth.

I saw myself
In Thay's Dharma talk in 2000
Dressed in an aspirant brown robe,
My hair in a bundle, full and black.

Who was that person?
Who is this person now, completely shaven?
Are they different from each other?
What have they gone through?

I saw monastic Sisters on stage
One looked just like me!
How could someone else look like me?
How could people mistake me for another?
Yet, at that moment,
I could mistake that Sister for me—
My face in the face of a Korean Sister
In a fifteen-year-old Sister
In a French Sister
In short and tall
Thin and chubby Sisters.
I saw sadness. I saw faith.
I saw a smile of pure joy.
I saw restlessness,
My face in their faces,
Looking at them. Being them.

In sitting meditation
My eyelids were closed,
Light particles can't penetrate them.
Yet, my inner eyes
Revealing to me
Images of my childhood
Of my young adulthood
Of my spirit path.

My inner eyes
Showing me

Interbeing
No need
To hide in shame
To flaunt in pride.

Never alone,
My faces are the faces of my Sisters,
Of partners, mother, grandmother,
Of leaves, mountains, memories,
Of awakened moments.

PUTTING ON THE SANGHATI

This brown robe is the earth,
This *sanghati* is the heaven,
These tears are the oceans,
A half smile cloaks the entire cosmos.

LOOKING AT THE ROSEBUD

I did not know it is this
Beautiful, but you always know
This rosebud, full of
Intricacies and simple beauties.

You envision it fully blooming,
While you, too, see the withering
And falling petals.

Fear, you have not.
You accept the nature of the rose,
As you see others continually
Bloom in its image.

BREATHE, MY CHILD

Breathe, breathe my child.
Let's breathe, breathe my child,
Thay teaches his children.
His words are sincere and dear,
Echoing in my deep slumber.
I wake up and come home.
Being near Thay, Sisters, and Brothers,
Each second, I breathe in their love.
Each small step, I let go of sadness.

Look at that tree,
Windstorms split in two,
Roots shredded and pulled,
Still holding on to brown earth.

Dear tree, I am like your trunk,
Battered by wind and rain, in birth and death.
This spring, the earth's calm, the sky's clear.
On the fresh branches, birds summon and sing.
Purple flowers dress this trunk with life.

HAPPINESS

Early spring evening,
High in the sky, a half-full moon.
I tilt my head to the moon,
Feeling the warm sunrays, the cool breeze,
Listening to cuckoo birds calling.
No happiness equals this.

ULTIMATE SELF

Sometimes I think I am a mighty wave,
Rising above all other waves.
Sometimes I think myself a forgotten wave,
Dying down before I am noticed.

Today, I am reminded that
My ultimate self is the water.
Higher waves, lower waves,
Large waves, single waves,
We all return to our ultimate self,

The water.

ALL THAT I HAVE

Don't take me to hell.   Let me stay
With the festive bird songs,   With my Sisters' laughter next door.

Let me stay   Watching the clouds floating, and
The occasional black birds   Zooming by the window
          On the rooftop.

Let me stay   With my laborious breathing
    From each beginning to each end.

Let me listen   To my heart beating.

Let me feel the pain of   My oral ulcers.

Let me stay here   With everything that I have.
Don't take me to hell.

PICKING AN ORACLE

Black copper
Round belly
Out of words
Full of emptiness.

REMAINING CLOSE

Happiness is something
Small and light,
Always remaining close to us.

When we quiet
Our mind and body
And listen,
We touch happiness
At once.

FROM THE HEART OF WINTER

Do you know when spring has come?
In the heart of the winter, life source continues to flow.
In the cutting cold, Mother Earth embraces seeds.
She nourishes barren branches.
Trees continue to breathe and
Prepare for their new coats,
So that today they manifest as spring.

Look, my love, look at the innumerable flowers and leaves.
Look, my love, look at yourself,
Your wonderful manifestations are all of this!
In the midst of suffering, of despair, of chaos,
Life source has never been absent in you.
Your loved ones are always there to guide you.
Each breath, each smile accumulates.
Each step in mindfulness is medicinal.
Each notion let go, each kind word,

All join in your life source,
So that today your spring manifests.

Look, my love, look at the innumerable flowers and leaves.
Look, my love, look at yourself,
Your wonderful manifestations are all of this!
Spring is coming, from the heart of the winter.

SING, SING, SING!

My lover goes to sea
Immersing his body in the powerful waves
There his spirit soars over
Timeless waters
Boundless mountains

His spirit sings
Music he is inspired to utter

DELIVERANCE

Teach me such simple beauty
Such magnificence
Such gentleness
Such loving kindness
You have taught me all that, and more.

The sun, the moon, the stars,
Do what they do,

Give what they give,
Not conscious of themselves.

Lunar eclipse, brilliant orange
Mixed yellow moon,
Veiled partially in quietude.
The stars in the sky light up,
Silvery bright, gentle,
Exuding beauty to all.

The bare winter trees
No longer bare.
Stars are their ornaments.

Just a taste
Of this on-going magical world
Fills me with deep gratitude.

Thank you, John.
As I become a nun,
In me, you become a monk,
Our spirits together
On the path of deliverance.

YOU BRING ME BACK

I love you. I love the spring—
Your deepened colors, butterflies, festive bird songs.
The young sheep frolic across
The lush green hills.

I love you. I love the summer—
The ardent light, fields of glowing sunflowers.
Lotuses bloom and fragrant the night,
Frogs' songs echo the stars and the moon.

I love you. I love the autumn—
Leaves return to the colors of their early beginnings.
Under the steps in walking meditation,
They rustle prayer songs.

I love you. I love the winter—
You continue to breathe with your denuded, gray body.
The song of impermanence lulls all species,
So that life's source flows freely.

I love you. You open this heart wide.
The whole universe enters each vein and artery.

I love you. My steps touch deeply the earth.
Mother's energy circulates in me.

I love you. You bring me back to the four seasons,
To the moon and the stars,
To the little sheep frolicking across the green hills.

STEPPING INTO FREEDOM

And like that I live joyfully each day,
And like that I let go each day,
And like that I see myself each day,
Happiness as well as sadness.

And like that I embrace myself each day,
And like that I take refuge in my Sisters each day,
And like that I join in each day,
With the rhythm of life, the sutras, the poems.

And like that I understand others more each day,
And like that the distance between us shortens,
And like that I come back to each day,
The breath, the smiles continue to radiate.

SONG OF RETURNING

In me, there is melancholy.
In me, there is a powerful chanting voice.
In me, there is a teardrop.
In me, there is light from the moon and stars.
In me, there is a harsh word.
In me, there is a reminder,
"Don't go there, my love."

In me, there is an upright row of coconut trees.
In me, there is a prayer.
In me, there is much unskillfulness and wrongdoing.
In me, there is shame at the sight of the moon.
In me, there is a cool, running river.
In me, there is a *coquelicot* with soft red petals.

In me is a thousand years of love and remembrance.
In me is the transmission of infinite generations.

What need is there to grasp?

TAKING A NAP IN THE HAMMOCK

Early summer day
Drops of sunlight swing the hammock.
Hands of leaves spread umbrellas.
The stream of birds orchestrates the breath.
The soul of poetry lulls sleep.

Ah, sleep my love, the light, gentle sleep.
I am still in you, in the breath short and long.
I am still in you, in the teardrops full and empty.
I am still in you, in the moments near and far.

Ah, smile my love, the wonderful smile.
The chestnut trees, with their roots penetrating
Deeply into the earth and their trunks posing
Still in the mid-sky,
Raise you high on the hammock
On an early summer day.

In a while, you will stretch your body.
Standing up, you carve my steps
On the thousand paths coming home.

RIVERS

Across the road from New Hamlet, my temple,
There is a river—
The river is of gigantic white plastic sheets
Covering long rows of earth mounds
To keep warm the asparagus seeds
During the winter months.

When spring arrives,
As dandelions blossom everywhere,
The asparagus, too, stretch up
And tear through the plastic sheets.
Groups of people will come to
Bathe in this river.
With one hand, they tear the plastic.
With the other, they dig up the asparagus,
Out of the earth.

I stand looking at the torn plastic river.
Years ago, my uncle's son drowned.
Since then, Grandmother forbade me from swimming.
But I loved rivers.
Many afternoons, I silently watched the waters,
Wishing to end my loneliness amidst this life.

Then my mother left one morning.
Her cream shirt became my last memory of her.
A plastic bag was seen floating
In a river near our house.
A woman was found inside, naked,
Tied by the hands and feet,
Crouched in a thick cloth sac,
Wrapped by a plastic bag outside.
Although Grandmother could not identify
The bloated body,
I quietly knew my mother's fate
Over these last twenty years.

But I loved the vast waters.
When my partner was taken away
By the currents, I could only beg:
Please, protect my loved one.

From the temple, the bell resounds calmly.
I embrace the rivers in me
With my quiet, regular breathing.
Soon, the harvest will be over.
The plastic pieces are removed.
The leftover asparagus
Stretch themselves in the spring light.
Their leaves are delicately long.
Their fruits are bright red, orange.
Then they dry up.
The seeds will be sown in
Rows of earth mounds,
Kept warm by gigantic plastic sheets.

These rivers
In motion over thousands of years
Suddenly arrest
When the temple bell
Calls me home.

SONG FOR MOTHER

This song is for you, my mother.
It has been a long time since I last saw you.
You were thirty-six when you walked
Out and never came back.
Now I am thirty-five, looking at myself
To find you.

This song is for you, my mother,
Whom I hated and blamed for
All my pain.

Now I learn to understand
Your suffering and embrace
Your struggles in me.

This song is for you, my mother,
Who gave me this beautiful smile,
This sadness,
This anger,
Who gave me this generosity,
Self-determination.

These vows I make to you, my mother:
All the beautiful seeds
You have planted in me,
I vow to cultivate and share.
All the negative traits
You have transmitted to me,
I vow to transform and
Heal, you in me.

PEANUT HEART

Oh, my peanut heart,
You are small, so you blame.
You are small, so you discriminate.
You are small, so you hold onto resentment.

Oh, my peanut heart,
Your volume is limited,
So back and forth you chew
The same things:
Reproaches and blaming.

You love, then you hate.
You hate, then you love.

Oh, my peanut heart,
Don't you see the deep red sun?
Don't you see the vast horizon?
Don't you see your teacher's love
Embracing all species?

I vow to breathe
When you contract.
I vow to see the beauty,
I vow to see the wholesomeness,
I vow to recognize the truth.

So you, my heart,
May open wide
To be stability.
Be peace.

So you, my heart,
May be the heart of the Buddha
Flowing with inclusiveness.
A life source.
A home for refuge.

STREAM ENTRY

Happiness is looking at me,
In the wind,
The rolling waves,
The rising sun.

Happiness is waving at me,
With the birds' wings,
My teacher's hands,
Each arriving footstep.

Happiness is embracing me,
Quiet and calm,
Full of gratitude,
Free of grasping.

Happiness is in my tear drops,
My pain,
Accepting,
No more running.

Happiness is you are me,
I am you,
Transforming together,
No discrimination.

Happiness is in just being,
Non-wishing,
Non-seeking,
Non-waiting.

Happiness is in sitting still,
Standing stably,
Breathing mindfully,
Doing nothing at all.

Happiness is here and now,
For you, for me,
Only if we are present
To be it.

BUDDHA AND MARA

These eyes have looked with compassion;
They have flashed in anger.

These ears have listened;
They have distorted.

This nose has recalled sweet memories;
It has deepened cravings.

This mouth has comforted;
It has destroyed.

This body has soared;
It has turned into stone.

This mind has run in darkness,
Now quieting.

STEP BY STEP

Sunshine on my face.
Sunshine on my shoulders.
Sunshine on my feet.

Let's walk in beauty, so all may be awakened.
Let's walk in wholesomeness, so all may see the way home.
Let's walk in truth, so all may arrive together.

Step by step, our feet touch the earth.
Step by step, breath is life.

WAVE AND THE OCEAN

I will tell you a story
About a wave and the ocean:
Since an unknown time
The wave feels all alone.
She searches for the ocean
In endless outward directions.

The wave is full of desires,
And the ocean is vast.
The wave keeps on looking,
But the ocean is still far, far away.

There are nights by the gentle moon
The wave holds herself in stillness.
Suddenly she feels immense.
The ocean whispers inside her.

Sometimes she also howls.
Raging in rapid successions,
She indulges in self-destruction,
Because ignorance from infinite time
Would not want to rest.

Only the wave understands
How vast the ocean is.
Only the ocean knows
Where the wave goes and returns to.

Those days when the wave vagabonds,
The ocean patiently awaits.
Those days when the wave plunges into despair,
The ocean continues to embrace.

If the wave sees the ocean
She would no longer need to search.

If you know that we are in one another
You will fear no more.

UNDER ONE ROOF

Smiling with the Buddha in me,
My mind suddenly lightens.
The curtain of despair draws close.
I see now! I understand now!

I see you, Mother, in your twenties,
Burdened by the family responsibilities.
Deep sadness lurked in your eyes.
Your body belonged to Father, and
You were fearful as the night came.
You begged for a little rest,
But Father kept tugging on your body.
I held my breath in the corner
Like a cockroach before a mouse.

I have carried your eyes into life.
My body has been abused by
Others' hands, and by my own.
The age of sixteen seems to drag on.
Sadness and despair surge up each day.
I cannot find comfort
Even in the thought of going to sleep,
Believing the situation will still be there
When I wake up.

Understanding with the Buddha's eye inside me,
I see that Mother is me.
I see that I am Mother.
Mother is not just suffering, and
I am not just despair.
Mother is an endless stream of love, as
I am a wonderful life source.
When I breathe, you rest.
When you smile, I have hope.

Loving with the Buddha's heart inside me,
I see that Father is me.
I see that I am Father.
Father is not just violent force, and
I am not just hatred.
Father has the seed of awakening,
As I have enlightenment in me.
When I am still, you stop.
When you come home, I am free.

I smile with you, Mother and Father.
Our family is under one roof.

WAITING TO DIE

Sometimes I sit waiting to die,
While marveling at the evening light glowing over treetops,
Watching an ant scurrying to and fro,
And listening to young birds' calls, near and far.

I know that life is like a waterfall.
My body grows older and weaker every moment.

I know that my own mind creates afflictions,
Grasping for rain bubbles this entire human life.

Still, sometimes I sit waiting to die.
Death sings each in-breath and out-breath!

Let the thoughts of love and rejection exhibit themselves.
Let the dust fly. Just watch it fly.
Keep on breathing, smiling, and waiting to die.
Be present to understand this "I" more.
Ah, the moment without waiting!
There is no coming, no going.

RECONCILIATION

"Would you like paper bags
Or plastic bags?"
I had asked a customer.

"What?" she seemed piqued.

Conscious of my accent,

I repeated my question
Slower, louder.

"What are you saying?" she retorted.
Disgusted, her upper lip curled
Her nose crunched up.

Pedaling home
In the dark, I cried.

I pledged: One day,
I'll be able to speak English fluently.
No one will insult me again.
No one!

Coming to America
For a better future at seventeen,
I said "Shit"
When I meant "sheet,"
"Bitch" instead of "beach."
In Miss Walske's ESL class,
We practiced with skits,
"Waiter, waiter,
There's a fly in my soup!"

On my first essay,
Mrs. Cummings wrote
"Fabw" everywhere.
I misread it as "Fabu"
Which must mean "fabulous"
Which she clarified,
"Find a better word."

My English teachers
Have since grown old
Or passed away

I've become a doctor
Then a nun,
Using my English
To share the Dharma
For the sake of
Many

EVENING SHADOW

Sitting here, observing a bird's shadow
On the mountain slope
I am the bird, soaring in the gentle breath
The bird is me, escaping from bondage
Open heart, empty hands, elated with the wind
A fading afternoon, a verdant afternoon.

Age is adding up quickly,
I'm already older than my mother!
The vast current of life blending
With the moon and wind

The bird's shadow is now gone,
The mountain ridge still standing
Who's coming
Who's going
On a verdant afternoon?

FLOWER OF COMPASSION

Love is a kind of flower
A flower that knows how to speak,
A flower that knows how to laugh,
A flower that knows how to bring joy,
Gently soothing wounds and bitterness.

A flower spreading in all directions
Free from boundaries and discrimination
Emanating rich fragrances and colors
Its broad wings embrace all with innocence.

My dear, you are a flower
In a wondrous garden of humanity
Live brightly and beautifully
So that your love overflows

A flower that never fades
Guiding you home in eternity
Love is a flower of compassion
Weaving the fabrics of life.

IMMENSITY

Is there an embrace wider than that of the universe?
Is there a love as vast as the love of Avalokiteshvara?
Is there any wisdom that shines as brightly as the wisdom of the
    Enlightened?
Is there any liberation as absolute as the liberation of the mind?

STOPPING

Coming back to this place
The city is bustling
But you are nowhere in sight.
Memories overflow with images,
Words, sounds rushing into the night
Tears soaking my pillow.

Your voice whispers:
Breathe, breathe, my dear.
Breathe, breathe, my love.

The wheels are still rolling
Yet my mind stops.
Stop, don't go back to the past
Chasing a shadow.
Stop, don't pursue the future
A fantasy.
I am staying here,
With everything within me,
At this moment.

Looking at my gentle teacher
A smile like a child
Hands etched with the months and years
Listening to the voice
Of understanding and love
My mind suddenly stops.

Stop, don't go back to the past
Chasing a shadow.
Stop, don't pursue the future
A fantasy.
I am staying here,
With everything within me,
At this moment.

LOVING ME

There are those who love me
Living true to their hearts
Sitting in silence
Listening to the wind
Smiling at the moon and stars.

There are those who love me
With tender hearts
Whether I'm beautiful or difficult
They are always by my side
Guiding my every step
Carrying me on their shoulders
When I fall in the dark of night.

There are those who love me
Giving me their own life
Now sitting quietly,
Listening to the wind,
I smile at the moon and stars.
Even their bodies may decay,
They live on within me
I vow to continue my beloved
Carrying them in my every step
The path ahead opens wide.

LOVE AWAKENED

You give me these gentle steps
You give me a powerful voice
You give a smile in the quiet night
You show a path to return to.

You give me infinite time
You give me the first love
You give me full embrace
You brighten my eyes with a full moon.

You are clouds, flowers, and leaves.
You are the moon, stars, and wind.
You are a pumpkin hanging heavy on the vine.

You are love awakened inside me
You are me, waking up from a deep dream
You are the Buddha, the Dharma, the Sangha.

HOME TO NON-WORRY

Sitting here looking at a tree,
The leaves are fluttering in the wind.

Sitting here in non-waiting,
With no regrets or worries.

Sitting here in eternity,
Tribulations of the years have passed.

Sitting here listening to you sing
The song of a brand-new morning—
    Many are waking up, rubbing their eyes,
    Stretching out their hands.

My love, sing the song of the morning.
Sing the song of non-waiting.
Sing, so the sun may radiate these moments,
    Coming home to non-worry.

DISCOURSE ON TRUE CONTENTMENT

*This poem was written together with my teacher, Thay
(Zen Master Thich Nhat Hanh), who graciously added to the
poem and edited it.*

I heard these words from Thay when he was staying at Deer Park
    Monastery.
Late at night, a group of coyotes appeared.
Their passionate howls made the whole Oak Grove tremble joyfully.
After paying respects to Thay with the right front paw pointing in the
    direction of the moon,
The elder coyote asked a question in the form of a verse:

People, animals, plants, and minerals are eager to know
What conditions lead to true contentment.
Please, Thay, will you teach us?

This is Thay's answer:

To live in a Sangha,
To have brothers and sisters working in harmony,
To serve peoples of all nations—
This is the true contentment.

To have a chance to practice and transform,
To see yourself becoming more accepting and more solid,
To recognize that others also blossom—
This is the true contentment.

To be able to reconcile and forgive,
To nurture gratitude to your blood family and spiritual family,
To express love through loving speech and deep listening—
This is the true contentment.

To have time to sit peacefully for your ancestors,
To touch the Earth tenderly with each step,
To eat mindfully in union with the whole cosmos—
This is the true contentment.

To create practice centers and hold regular retreats,
To turn gymnasiums and theaters into Dharma halls,
To bring the Dharma rain into ghettos and prisons—
This is the true contentment.

To witness police officers, business people, legislators,
Scientists, and war veterans enjoying the Pure Land
With their mindful breath and mindful steps—
This is the true contentment.

To provide a joyful environment for young people,
To help them reconnect with their families and society,
To show them that there is a beautiful path—
This is the true contentment.

To practice, work, study, and play together,
To be aware of the beauties and hardships of your brothers and sisters,
To cherish and protect them as your own marrow—
This is the true contentment.

To live a life simple and uncompetitive,
To come back to your breath as your soul food,
To rejoice in the music of the bell, wind songs, and laughter—
This is the true contentment.

To avoid speaking and reacting in anger,
Not caught by your ideas and judgments,
And to be diligent in beginning anew—
This is the true contentment.

To savor the freedom in non-waiting,
To transform the grasping mind into that of true love,
To be a kind continuation of your spiritual ancestors—
This is the true contentment.

To see all life forms as your brothers and sisters,
To enjoy simply be-in together,
To actively build a beautiful past with your true presence—
This is the true contentment.

To rise in the morning with a smile,
To retire each night with peace, content to let go of all,
To know that you have loved and been loved deeply—
This is the true contentment.

To live in the world
With your heart open to impermanence and change,
To progress stably on your true path, free of fear and worry—
This is the true contentment.

For he or she who accomplishes this,
Arriving and at home wherever she goes,
Always he is peaceful and happy—
True contentment is in the moment one lives.

INSIGHT GATHA

A flower falls, thousands continuing.
A song fades, birds singing out of space.
The heart of love illuminates in the sea of fire,
Fulfilling its vow with the ancient moon.

A SISTER'S LOVE

As loving a sister as I am,
I cannot take away your sickness
But help you care for it.
I cannot remove your darkness
But soothe your heart with deep listening.

I cannot stop death
At the moment it lifts your life
But I can be there to guide you
Through your last breath

As I have been there to embrace
Tragedy and laughter
Your whole life.

REBIRTH

I have died in the ocean, towered by waves.
I have died at the bottom of a sharp cliff.
I have died in the midst of lonely nights.
I have died on my knees on the sidewalk.

I have died and have been reborn,
Brand new like a baby with breath
Still fragrant of mother's milk.
There is laughter in each discovering step.

I have returned to be the child of earth and sky,
Full of wildflowers and dancing grass.

TUCKED IN

Sunrays
Shine through
Stormy wind
Wintery air

My dear head's
Hurting
Spinning

I lie down
Tucked in
By sunrays

STILL HERE

I wrote my best poem
In my sleep.
I know it because
I told myself so.

I wrote my best song
In my dream.
I even tried
To memorize it.

But I forgot
The words the moment
I woke up.

So I do my best to live
My ordinary life

Through each breath, however comfortable
Or shortened it may be—
In this body, although pain
And weariness can be relentless at times—
In each interaction, knowing it's the last—
Holding and embracing gently,
Tears and laughter.

And I have touched the most
Exquisite love
In these wakeful moments.

CHILD FRIEND

You come night
After night.
"Anyone there?"
"Want to play?"
You call out,
Joyfully leading the way.

You are my child friend
And in you,
My child self is revealed,
Ready for adventure,
For joy—

"You are so childish!" you exclaim.
"You are so immature!" I reply.
Then we hop and
Skip into
Light.

PINE TREE IN THE FRONT GATE

Have you seen the pine tree in front of the gate?
Standing tall and proud, swaying in the high sky
Through four seasons, in snow and scorching sun
Always green, embracing countless beings.

Be like the pine tree in front of the gate,
Standing tall and proud, swaying in the high sky
Through four seasons, in snow and scorching sun
Always shining the beginner's mind.

CALLING YOUR NAME

I call your name,
The long winding forest path murmurs.
I call your name,
Leaves falling or sunlight sketching in space.
I call your name,
Water flowing endlessly past the rocks.
I call your name,
Each step is endearing!

Suddenly,
The sound of you calling me back,
Eternity in birdsongs!

INTERDEPENDENCE

The sun our heart
The forest our lungs
The river our bloodstream
Breathing through countless generations
Protecting all life force.

HOME

May I choose this breath as my home
May I choose these steps as my home
May I choose this smile as my home
May I accept Mother Earth as my home
This breath is my home
These steps are my home
This smile is my home
This Earth is my home
There is only home
Only home
Home

TOUCH THE EARTH

Touch the Earth
For sunlight to shine through
For wholesome seeds to sprout
For a child's eyes in a war zone to brighten

Touch the Earth
For shattered trunks to put on new coats
For a lullaby to cool the desert
Shading and protecting

Touch the Earth
Listen to the waves laughing
Listen to flowers dancing
Listen to cries deep within

Touch the Earth
Be still in the raging fire
On the face hollow of life

Touch the Earth
Look deep in the eyes
Listen to rainstorms dissolving in the sea

Touch the Earth once
For hatred to dissipate
Years of holding to blocks of pain

Touch the Earth
For love to deepen
For mothers to smile
For transmission to be possible

Touch the Earth closely
For the steps to lighten
For love to heal the land's sorrow

Touch the Earth deeply
Let Mother Earth embrace us

A hundred years of tears
Suddenly turn to light

Touch the Earth
For love to ignite
For brotherhood and sisterhood to strengthen
To keep a place warm
For the wounded to come home

Touch the Earth
The meadow is luscious
Songs are soaring
Raindrops dancing

Peace is this beautiful path
Peace is home
For all

DRINK YOUR TEA

Drink your tea
Drink the cloud
Drink the rain
Drink the melodious river

Drink your tea
Drink time
Drink the great Earth
Drink birth and death

Live authentically
Live beautifully
Live wholesomely

Tomorrow you will leave
Where will you be going?

Going to make clouds
To make rain
To high mountains
To the vast sea

Drink your tea!

DRUM OF GREAT COMPASSION

Live for me
Speak for me
Breathe for me

These hands are mother's hands
Providing tenderness
Bringing hope
Fulfilling a child's dream

Live for me
Speak for me
Breathe for me

This heart is Thay's heart
Calling for peace
For peoples to find home

In one another

Who can hear
The drum of great compassion?

Leave behind hatred and fear
Walk together
Warm hands in synchronous beats

Live together
Speak to each other
Breathe with one another

In the flower of nondiscrimination
These hands
These heartbeats
Have no coming
No going.

FOLLOWING YOUR FOOTSTEPS

Allow me to kiss your feet
Those delicate feet
Doing walking meditation
All over the five continents
Helping peoples cross
The shore of suffering

Footsteps transmitting love
Kissing Mother Earth
Healing wounds
Flowers blooming everywhere

Footsteps carrying peace
Into dark places
Engaging in the world
Love for humanity

Allow me to kiss your feet
Those small feet
Doing walking meditation
All over the five continents
Helping peoples cross
The shore of suffering

Footsteps bearing good news
Everyone is waiting for
Light like breath
Powerful as waves

Allow me to follow your footsteps
To return to my true home
One step continuing the other
Without beginning
Without end

GREAT TEMPLE BELL

The nightly temple bell
Tolling through mountains and the city below,
Dispelling sadness and despair,
Awakening beings from their slumber,
"Who's coming? Who's going?"

The nightly temple bell
Tolling through mountains and the city below
Marking the passing of another lifetime,
Resounding the old vows,
Forgotten in endless wandering, drifting like shadows.

Eyes of the thousand stars
Illuminating humanity
Lighting up the homeward path
Silent mind recognizes the ancient place.

Countless beings are caught
In their own karmas and dramas.
Purifying one's actions brings awakening to others.

The bell toll tonight is tranquil
Like a rest note,
Familiar like mother's scent.

In just a moment,
All worries slough off.

TRUE CONTENTMENT

Seeing clearly the situation
Casting away all grasping and hatred
Smiling in those last moments

Truly content.
What's more to wish for?

EARTHLY JOURNEY

In forgetfulness,
I've wandered through life.
Now I'm returning
To surrender at your feet.
Impermanence has descended
Suddenly upon me.

Tossed in the sea of sorrow and regret,
I am small and helpless.
Please protect my beloved!

For the sake of fame,
I chased after degrees and titles,
Turning my back to the present moment
Lost in winning and losing.
My beloved was there,
But invisible to me.

Time and time again,
My thoughts were filled with judgment,
Blaming others for not understanding me
Then harsh words, then cold silence,
Rejecting what was once cherished
Love once precious now a burden
Home once cozy now devoid.

Dear Buddha,
Please sprinkle light into my erring heart
Save your lost child
Allow me a moment of rest
Help me to fight no more.

I'm learning
To breathe, to smile,
To walk, to stand, to look deeply.
My beloved is always here
Manifesting in the vibrant tapestry of life.

I live beautifully
My love lives on beautifully.
Building the past in today
Living mindfully every moment
Is to see that nothing is lost.

How miraculous is this spiritual path!
Filled with gratitude,
I touch the Earth
Before countless Buddhas.

WHOLENESS

With utmost humility,
I prostrate on the Earth
Gentle mother
Nurturing my life force,
Providing me a place to lean on,
Steadying my steps.

Whenever I feel sad,
Swept by anger,
Drowned in self-destruction,
All I need to do is
To listen to my breathing,

To take mindful steps,
To sit with upright posture,
To lay down my body.

In that instant
Mother Earth envelopes me
In her steadfast peace.
Mother, help me calm the storms within,
Transmit to me the ability to transform unskillfulness
So that flowers may bloom tomorrow
Adorning life with beauty.

My mind, like the Earth,
Contains countless seeds,
Sown and cultivated over lifetimes.
I vow to nurture
Seeds of understanding and compassion.
I vow to transform
Seeds of suffering,
So that my ancestors
May continue beautifully.

Mother Earth bore witness
To the Buddha's enlightenment.
Mother Earth gave birth
To countless Great Beings.

I return to the Earth,
My mind is the Earth,
The earth is my true nature.

I have arrived.
I am whole.

DON'T WAIT

If you want a spiritual life,
Then live it right now.
Don't wait till tomorrow,
When your body is weary.
Don't wait till tomorrow,
You'll be ashes.

Youth is like wings of a butterfly,
Days passing through storms and tempests.
Do you know what to do,
Or you're just waiting and hoping?

If you want to love,
Then cultivate understanding.
Don't seek the future in fame and wealth.
Don't place anyone in bondage.

Love is like a leaf
Drifting in the wind.
What is there to grasp?

My dear, the authentic person
Is you in this moment
Smiling with non-fear,
Expecting nothing, asking for nothing.
Each step is taken with leisure,
What is there to exploit?

Day after day,
You are singing,
Your love deepening,
Fulfilling your ancient vows.

SWEET EARTH

Where are you now?
What are you doing?
You heard the call of your heart,
Waking up with an open heart.
No more searching.
No more feeling lost.
You wanted to come home,
Your eyes shone brightly.

Autumn has passed,
Then came winter,
Now flowers fan over sweet Earth.

I'm still silently waiting
For your return.

LOVE LETTER TO MY BROTHER

This love letter is for you,
The one I've cherished since the first time I laid eyes on.
You were tiny, nestled in the hammock
In front of our ancestral home.
Our cousin, Anh Ty, hung a round beetle on a string
Between the two ends of the hammock.
Every time he swung the hammock,
The wind made the beetle spread its wings,
Its buzzing sound made you chuckle joyfully.

This love letter is for you,
The boy I carried on my shoulders on the way home from school,
Teaching you to count from one to forty.
One day, you leaped onto my back as usual,
My knees buckled and
I realized that my little brother had grown up—
I could no longer cradle or carry you anymore!

This love letter is for you,
My loyal friend, confiding in me all your joys and sorrows,
Your first loves and those most embarrassing moments.
Later I reminded you of them,
You became even more embarrassed:
"Did I really tell you that?
No, I couldn't have told you that!"

This love letter is for you,
My savior, my life thread.
In many moments of despair, I wanted to end it all,
But your image appeared.
I couldn't bear to leave you behind.
My pain and shortcut would forever fester in you.

There were times you sat with a gun pointed at your temple,
But you thought of me.
You couldn't leave me wandering alone in this world.
Every time I cried, you cried along,
Whether you knew why I cried or not.
Even now, we are both older,
Whenever I start to sniffle, you plead:
"Oh, please, don't do that! Don't cry, sister!
I'll do anything for you to be happy."

My love, thirty-some years have passed in the blink of an eye.
My little brother has grown into a handsome, kind-hearted person—
Responsible, polite, affectionate, always ready to help others.
I am so happy and proud of you!
Surely, every time Mother looks down from heaven,
She says: "My golden nugget is most precious!"
Surely, Grandma smiles, her eyes squinting like a comet.

My love, when you visited me at the University of San Diego,
You were laughing and chatting with my monastic Brothers and Sisters
    so naturally.
My heart was filled with joy.
You have accepted and appreciated the people I leaned on.
You have begun to understand why I chose this path.

Every day, I remind myself:
I cultivate inner peace to pave the way for you to come back.
I look in such a way that your eyes may brighten,
For you to see the cosmic wonder within you.
I smile so that your lips as rosy as lotus petals,
Nurture joy and hope in your heart.
I walk with awareness so that you may stop longing, stop searching,
And let go of all bitterness.
I love you not only through words and gestures,
But my own life is a life force within you.

This love letter is for you
On the occasion of the Rose for Your Pocket Ceremony.
I pin this rose on your lapel with a prayer
That our mutual maternal love and siblinghood
Will always illuminate our life journey together.

THIRTY-SIX-YEAR ANNIVERSARY

I am thirty-six today.

Mother, at the age of thirty-six,
You had two children,
An old husband,
Many ambitions,
Worries,
Anger,
Pain.

I am more fortunate than you.
I can take peaceful steps.
I have a chance to sit still.
No one is toiling with my body.
I marvel at the autumn light.

You thought of ways to get more from life.
I ask myself: How can I stop?

Mother, my life is because your life was.
I take these peaceful steps for you.
I sit still for you.
I heal this body for you.

The gentle light traverses infinite time.

BELOVED

You sit down
After having come and gone,

Lost in passion, drifted in the abyss of regret and sorrow.
You sit down,
Your body stable and tranquil—
Such beautiful posture
Bringing you back to this serene moment.
No longer seeking.

You sit down
And there is stability in life.
Fires of pain blossom into a lotus pond.
Your heart heals from wounds of hatred.
From this moment on, life reclaims you,
Like a soaring bird,
Like the sea's lullaby.
Although your body comes and goes,
These moments become eternal autumn.

The sun is still here, bestowing life upon you.
Mother Earth is still here, cradling you.
Love sweetly shields ripe autumn leaves.

Your past vows echo in endless waves.
You sit and listen deeply.
Who is the beloved?
After all these years,
You have returned!

You sit down, here,
Touching the core of the Earth,
The beating rhythm of birds' wings,
Home.

In the quiet morning,

The great temple bell tolls in intervals
We sit down together
To illuminate inner peace, to bring joy to life.

SIMPLY BE

For so many years
I yearned for you
I thought of you each
And every day
In the midst of busyness
In the midst of joy
In the midst of solitude

Like something dropped
Suddenly
Into a deep
Hollow well
Reverberating
Stirring
Unquenchable

Now there is no thought of you
I am glad!

There is no yearning for you
I am thankful!

I can be
With what is

Simply be.

LIFE OF PEACEFUL ROAMING

"A life of peaceful roaming,"
The phrase kept repeating in my dream,
Even as I woke up.

No, I am not dreaming.
This is my life.
Gone is the life full of struggles,
Ongoing drama,
Endless trauma.
Done is the constant craving
For acknowledgement,
Love, and acceptance,
A place in the world.

Now I dwell in my breathing,
At home in my body,
A constant companion,
A soulmate to myself

Peaceful roaming
Peaceful dwelling
Wherever I go.

MY ROBE

In my dream
An important event is
About to take place,
Perhaps my own wedding.
I have to choose what to wear.

One gown after another,
Beautiful, exotic,
Yet none feel befitting.

Such uncertainty!
Such dissatisfaction!

Then finally,
Standing at the center,
Surrounded by spectators

All alone

Cloaked in my brown monastic robe,
I feel most at ease.
Free!

SUDDEN QUERY

Where are you hurrying to
So early in the morning,
Late at night,
At midday?

While sweet bird songs,
Brilliant flowers
Display
Life's wonders

Everywhere.

TWO WAYS

There are two ways to
Respond to hurtful actions

One is to lash out
In retaliation

The other
To lay low,
Even for one breath,
With a half smile—

Choosing
To be free.

THAY'S LEGACY

You leave us your footsteps in meditation
Your graceful, non-fear smile
Cozy, intimate moments
Guiding us through life with unwavering faith.

You remind us
Today is beautiful!
Young shoots stretching in the morning sun
A small rabbit happily nibbling on grass
The silhouette of green mountains amidst the clouds.

You leave us enchanting moonlit nights
Words of confidence and trust
Boundless love and affection

You lead us to our
Original grace
Carefree innocence.

TO BE FREE

Treasure
What didn't happen.

Release
What happened.

Be
Light.

AGING

The more
White hair I have

The more often
I shave my head

Vain,
I still am!

HUMAN-CAUSED CONDITIONS

Trees bend and
Twist their
Roots, trunks,
Branches, stems
Unimaginably
In all sorts of
Forms in order to
Rise
Upward
To meet the sun.

People bend and
Distort
Only to descend
Into despair,
Darkness,
Hell realms

Pulling humans,
Other species,
Along with them.

NON-SELF

Under the shower head
Warm water flowing

Utterly naked
Exposed to the core
Breathing

My weary body dissolves
My frozen heart thaws

Slowly
Slowly

Only water is left
Going down the drain
To the sewage
Onward to the river
Back to the sea

SLOUGHING OFF

These days I enjoy
Lying on a hammock
My body curls
Like a fetus, gently swaying
In Mother Earth's womb
All my doings slough off
I
simply
be

STOPPING

Yet another dream
Trying to leave here
To go somewhere
Safer, better

Running late again
Panic
Scattered

People all around
Yet distant
Unreal

Suddenly
A thought arose,
No need to go
Anywhere
I'm already
There!

The hubbub
Vanished

Utterly still.

PERCEPTION–DECEPTION

Something
Is
Crawling
Between my toes

Nothing
No crawling
Sensations
    Only

Scratch
It intensifies

Be still
It subsides

Such is the mind!
Such is life!

LIFE WITHOUT BOUNDARIES

Safe to myself
I am safe to the world.
    At ease in myself
    I am at ease in the world.
At home in myself
I am at home in the world.
    Healing myself
    Is healing you
    Deep within.

FAREWELL SMILE

"What would be your last words
If you were to die today?"
My sister asked me,
Eyes clear and curious.

A smile
On my lips

Is
Enough.

No wish to be somewhere else
To do anything else.

At peace if there's someone
Or no one
With me
At my deathbed.

FEATHER ON A MIDDAY

If I had not stopped to watch
A feather coasting by,
I would not have seen its landing—
A tiny, pure white, fine feather.

Gently, I blew a soft breath to send it
Back to the spring.

If I had not looked up to watch
The feather gliding over the roof,
I would not have seen
The crescent moon hanging
At midday.

GATHAS
(Practice Poems)

A *gatha* is a short verse or poem that is used in mindfulness practice to intertwine spirituality and everyday living. These verses serve as gentle reminders to return to the present moment. They are imbued with the essence of mindfulness and are designed to transform mundane activities into moments of spiritual practice and awareness.

I offer you these gathas, fruits of my healing process, in the hopes that they may be a profound yet simple way to cultivate mindfulness and presence in your daily life. I have found that intentionally reciting a gatha, either aloud or silently, as I do a certain activity helps to bring me into the moment. I like to then pause to notice, perhaps there are changes in my awareness or attitude toward the activity I am engaged in. Over time, this practice can transform any task into an opportunity for awareness and ease. Of course, you can engage with these gathas in your own creative way, and I encourage you to write your own gathas as you move through your day.

GATHA ON PUTTING ON CLOTHES

Putting on my clothes,
I am grateful to all beings who are protecting me.
I carry the Three Jewels to guard my six senses.

GATHA FOR WASHING HANDS

Washing my hands,
I remove my three karmic actions
Of body, speech, and mind.
Seeing that my body is temporary,
I vow to practice even more diligently.

GATHA FOR BRUSHING TEETH

I've been given this day,
To have teeth to brush.
To have reasons to smile.

GATHA FOR STANDING UP

Standing up, I know that I am standing up.
I follow the Buddha and Thay
To go in the upward direction.

GATHA FOR GOING TO SLEEP

I vow to bring awareness
Into my sleep this night,
To dispel all fears,
To see emptiness in all desires,
To find my way out with mindfulness,
To know what is reality, what is illusory.

GATHA FOR LISTENING TO BIRDS SINGING

The birds are singing Dharma songs:
All things are here.
Our loved ones are always in us.
We only need to be present
To be united and happy.

GATHA FOR WALKING IN THE RAIN

This morning I walk,
Raindrops continue my footsteps.
Each drop of rain
Deepens my gratitude.

GATHA BEFORE STUDYING OR READING

Please help me to learn so that I may communicate,
Understand, and love others better.
I do not learn to feed my ego.
Knowledge has never brought me true happiness.

GATHA FOR REMEMBERING OUR INTENTION

How great is the life of a practitioner!
Unperturbed amidst waves and winds
Shaking off worldly attachment
Continuing our spiritual legacy.

GATHA FOR TRANSFORMING HABITS

The sea does not purge carcasses
Carcasses actually drift into shore.
The Sangha does not abandon its members
Our negative habits steer us from the path.

GATHA FOR SITTING MEDITATION

Calm mind, calm breathing
Calm breathing, still mind
Body, mind, and breath
Neither one
Nor three.

GATHA FOR REFLECTING ON UNSKILLFUL SPEECH

I still boast, showing off with pride,
Exaggerating, minimizing, flaunting my achievements.
Knowing that I am wrong, I still go on talking.
Got it! Got it!
Why keep on talking,
Causing myself more misery?

GATHA FOR TAKING CARE OF OUR BODY

This body is the body of my ancestors, containing all wisdom and
potential for liberation.
May I live with full awareness of my body so that healing and trans-
formation may take in place every moment.

Acknowledgments

I would never have written this book, or experienced the healing contained in its pages, without the support and encouragement of many people along the way.

My deep gratitude to my high school teachers, in particular Ms. Walske and Mrs. Cummings at Marcos de Niza, and my college professors, especially Naomi and Martha at the University of Arizona, who spent endless hours tutoring me and encouraged me so passionately that I ended up with a Bachelor of Arts degree in creative writing! Martha was the person in my life who told me that my writing was "unique" and "had substance," even while I still struggled with writing in English as a second language.

I also wish to express my gratitude to Hisae Matsuda for her appreciation and confidence in my poetry, which has now manifested as this collection. Thank you, Hisae, and thank you to Parallax Press editor Miranda Perrone, for all your crucial work.

I owe my spiritual life and healing to my beloved teacher, Zen Master Thich Nhat Hanh. Thank you for encouraging me to continue to write after receiving my letter sharing my life journey. Your enthusiastic reception of my first article recounting the story of a twelve-year-old girl whom I was taking care of as a novice helped me to trust myself and my expressive ability. Thank you, Thay, for all your love, guidance, and support.

About Sister Dang Nghiem

Sister Dang Nghiem, MD, a Vietnamese-American Zen Buddhist nun, is a disciple of the revered Zen Master Thich Nhat Hanh. Born in 1968 in Vietnam during the Tet Offensive, she is a prominent figure in contemporary Buddhist practice. Her journey as the daughter of a Vietnamese mother and an American soldier is marked by profound personal losses and challenges, which she transformed into the foundation of her spiritual path. She lost her mother at the age of twelve and immigrated to the United States at the age of seventeen with her younger brother. Living in various foster homes, she learned English and went on to earn a medical degree from the University of California San Francisco, during which time she was awarded a William Carlos Williams Poetry Award for her poem "Grandma."

After suffering further tragedy and loss, she quit her practice as a doctor to travel to Plum Village monastery in France, founded by Zen Master Thich Nhat Hanh, where she was ordained as a nun in 2000. She is the author of three books: a memoir, *Healing: A Woman's Journey from Doctor to Nun* (2010); *Mindfulness as Medicine: A Story of Healing and Spirit* (2015); and *Flowers in the Dark: Reclaiming Your Power to Heal from Trauma with Mindfulness* (2021). Her work focuses on the intersection of personal healing and spiritual growth, drawing from her unique experiences as a physician, a nun, and an individual who has navigated diverse worlds. Sister Dang Nghiem's ability to articulate the complexities of human suffering and the path to inner peace makes her a resonant voice in modern spirituality.

Monastics and visitors practice the art of mindful living in the tradition of Thich Nhat Hanh at our mindfulness practice centers around the world. To reach any of these communities, or for information about how individuals, couples, and families can join in a retreat, please contact:

PLUM VILLAGE
33580 Dieulivol, France
plumvillage.org

LA MAISON DE L'INSPIR
77510 Villeneuve-sur-Bellot, France
maisondelinspir.org

HEALING SPRING
MONASTERY
77510 Verdelot, France
healingspringmonastery.org

MAGNOLIA GROVE
MONASTERY
Batesville, MS 38606, USA
magnoliagrovemonastery.org

BLUE CLIFF MONASTERY
Pine Bush, NY 12566, USA
bluecliffmonastery.org

DEER PARK MONASTERY
Escondido, CA 92026, USA
deerparkmonastery.org

EUROPEAN INSTITUTE OF
APPLIED BUDDHISM
D-51545 Waldbröl, Germany
eiab.eu

THAILAND PLUM VILLAGE
*Nakhon Ratchasima
30130 Thailand*
thaiplumvillage.org

ASIAN INSTITUTE OF
APPLIED BUDDHISM
Lantau Island, Hong Kong
pvfhk.org

STREAM ENTERING
MONASTERY
*Beaufort, Victoria 3373
Australia*
nhapluu.org

MOUNTAIN SPRING
MONASTERY
Bilpin, NSW 2758, Australia
mountainspringmonastery.org

For more information visit: *plumvillage.org*
To find an online sangha visit: *plumline.org*
For more resources, try the Plum Village app: *plumvillage.app*
Social media: *@thichnhathanh @plumvillagefrance*

PARALLAX PRESS, a nonprofit publisher founded by Zen Master Thich Nhat Hanh, publishes books and media on the art of mindful living and Engaged Buddhism. We are committed to offering teachings that help transform suffering and injustice. Our aspiration is to contribute to collective insight and awakening, bringing about a more joyful, healthy, and compassionate society.

View our entire library at parallax.org.

THE MINDFULNESS BELL is a journal of the art of mindful living in the Plum Village tradition of Thich Nhat Hanh. To subscribe or to see the worldwide directory of Sanghas (local mindfulness groups), visit mindfulnessbell.org.